Artificial Intelligence and Customer Equity

Driving Business Success and Business Growth Through AI

KONSTANTIN TITOV

ISBN: 979-8-3440-3089-0

TABLE OF CONTENTS

CHAPTER 1

A MARKETING PERSPECTIVE FOCUSED ON THE CUSTOMER

In today's competitive business world, a customer-centric approach to marketing has become a critical factor for success. Companies are realizing that focusing on their customers, rather than just on their products or services, is key to long-term growth and profitability.

This shift represents a deeper understanding of customer needs, behaviors, and preferences. In this chapter, we will explore what it means to have a customer-focused marketing perspective and why it matters now more than ever.

The Evolution of Marketing

Traditionally, marketing was product driven. Companies would develop products and then use marketing tactics to sell them to as many people as possible.

This approach centered on the product's features and benefits, with little regard for what customers wanted. It was more about pushing sales than building relationships.

However, the business landscape has changed. Customers are now more empowered than ever, with access to endless information and choices. They no longer passively accept marketing messages.

Instead, they actively research, compare, and make decisions based on their own needs and values. As a result, companies had to adapt by shifting their focus from products to customers. This is where customer-centric marketing comes in.

What Is Customer-Centric Marketing?

Customer-centric marketing means placing the customer at the core of all marketing strategies. It involves understanding customer needs, preferences, and pain points and designing products, services, and experiences around them. The goal is not just to sell products but to build lasting relationships that foster loyalty and advocacy.

In customer-centric marketing, businesses create personalized experiences for their customers. This requires collecting data on customer behavior and using that data to tailor interactions. With the rise of digital tools and artificial intelligence (AI), it has become easier than ever to gather and analyze customer data, making personalization a key strategy for companies aiming to enhance customer satisfaction.

Why a Customer-Centric Approach Matters

A customer-focused marketing strategy offers many benefits for businesses, particularly in today's highly competitive and saturated market. Here are some reasons why adopting a customer-centric perspective is crucial:

Improved Customer Loyalty: When companies focus on meeting customer needs and delivering value, they naturally foster loyalty. Satisfied customers are more likely to return for future purchases and recommend the brand to others. Customer loyalty leads to repeat business, which is often more cost-effective than acquiring new customers.

Increased Customer Lifetime Value (CLV): Customer-centric marketing helps businesses maximize the lifetime value of each customer. By nurturing customer relationships, companies can encourage repeat purchases and upselling opportunities. The longer a customer stays loyal to a brand, the more profitable they become over time.

Enhanced Customer Experience: A customer-centric approach aims to create positive experiences at every stage of the customer journey. Whether it's through personalized product recommendations, responsive customer service, or user-friendly interfaces, focusing on the customer's experience can lead to higher satisfaction and better retention.

Brand Differentiation: In a crowded market, a customer-first approach helps brands stand out. By offering tailored experiences and showing genuine care for customers, companies can differentiate themselves from competitors who focus only on product features or pricing.

Better Customer Insights: When businesses focus on their customers, they gain valuable insights into what drives purchasing decisions.

This data can be used to refine marketing strategies, develop better products, and offer more relevant content, resulting in stronger connections with the target audience.

How to Implement a Customer-Centric Marketing Strategy

Developing a customer-centric marketing strategy requires a deep understanding of your audience and a commitment to putting their needs at the center of your efforts. Below are some key steps to implementing a successful customer-focused marketing approach.

Understand Your Customers: The first step to adopting a customer-centric approach is to truly understand who your customers are. This involves conducting market research, collecting customer feedback, and analyzing data to identify customer segments, behaviors, and preferences. By building detailed customer personas, you can ensure that your marketing efforts align with the unique needs and desires of different segments of your audience.

Personalize Your Marketing: Personalization is at the heart of customer-centric marketing. With AI tools and customer data analytics, businesses can now offer highly tailored experiences. This could be as simple as addressing customers by their names in emails or as complex as providing customized product recommendations based on past purchases. Personalization helps create a stronger emotional connection with customers and makes them feel valued.

Create Customer-Centric Content: Content marketing plays a significant role in a customer-focused strategy. To engage your audience, the content must resonate with their needs and pain points.

Create educational, entertaining, or problem-solving content that addresses the issues your customers care about. This positions your brand as a helpful resource, which builds trust and credibility over time.

Deliver Exceptional Customer Service: A big part of being customer-centric is providing excellent customer service. Every interaction with your brand should reflect your commitment to customer satisfaction. Whether it's through quick response times, friendly support staff, or easy returns policies, showing that you care about your customers' experiences will boost loyalty and satisfaction.

Collect and Act on Feedback: Customer feedback is a valuable resource for improving your marketing and overall business strategy. Regularly collect feedback through surveys, reviews, and social media interactions.

Use this feedback to improve your offerings and address any pain points that customers may have. When customers see that their opinions matter and lead to positive changes, they are more likely to stay loyal to your brand.

Leverage Technology and Data: To truly excel at customer-centric marketing, you need to make use of technology and data analytics. AI-driven tools can help businesses collect and analyze large volumes of customer data.

This data can be used to better understand customer preferences and predict future behaviors, allowing for even more personalized and effective marketing efforts. Additionally, automation tools can help businesses streamline their processes, ensuring consistent and relevant communication with customers.

Challenges of a Customer-Centric Approach

While the benefits of a customer-centric marketing strategy are clear, there are also challenges that businesses must overcome to successfully implement this approach. One of the main challenges is gathering and managing customer data effectively. With the growing concern over data privacy, companies need to ensure they are transparent about data collection practices and comply with regulations like GDPR.

Another challenge is aligning the entire organization with a customer-centric mindset. It's not just the marketing department that needs to focus on the customer; every department, from sales to product development to customer service, should work towards creating positive customer experiences. This often requires a cultural shift within the organization.

A marketing perspective focused on the customer is no longer an option — it's a necessity for businesses looking to thrive in today's market.

By putting customers at the center of your marketing strategy, you can build stronger relationships, foster loyalty, and create meaningful experiences that drive long-term growth. Embrace personalization, listen to feedback, and use technology to understand your customers better.

In doing so, you will not only meet their expectations but exceed them, ensuring your brand remains relevant and competitive for years to come.

CHAPTER 2

LINKING CUSTOMER EQUITY TO BUSINESS VALUE

In today's competitive market, businesses need to measure success beyond short-term profits. Focusing on customer equity allows companies to understand their true value by building lasting relationships with their customers.

Customer equity reflects the total value a business derives from its customers over time. By linking customer equity to business value, organizations can shift their focus from immediate gains to long-term growth and sustainability.

This chapter explores how companies can connect customer equity to their business value, why it's important, and how businesses can leverage this concept for success.

What is Customer Equity?

Customer equity is the total lifetime value of a company's customer base. It's not just about the number of customers or the revenue they generate today. Instead, customer equity considers the entire customer lifecycle — from the moment a customer first interacts with a brand to their repeated transactions over time.

Three core components drive customer equity:

Value Equity: The perceived value of the product or service.
Brand Equity: The value customers associate with a brand based on their experiences and perceptions.
Retention Equity: The customer's likelihood of staying loyal to a brand and continuing to make purchases.

These elements combine to form customer equity, which gives businesses a clear picture of their long-term value.

Why Linking Customer Equity to Business Value Matters

Linking customer equity to business value is essential for several reasons. First, it shifts the company's mindset from short-term profits to long-term success.

While one-off sales may provide a temporary revenue boost, businesses need sustainable, loyal customers to thrive over time. Focusing on customer equity ensures companies build relationships that last, creating consistent revenue streams.

Second, customer equity offers a more comprehensive way to measure a company's health. Financial reports may show profit and loss statements, but they don't always reflect the strength of customer relationships.

Businesses with high customer equity have loyal customers who continue to provide value, even in challenging times. This stability can be a key factor in securing investments or driving company growth.

Finally, customer equity serves as a leading indicator of business success. By focusing on the lifetime value of their customers, businesses can predict future revenue and make smarter strategic decisions. Companies with strong customer equity tend to have higher market valuations because they have built a base of loyal customers who will continue to contribute to revenue.

Measuring Customer Equity

To effectively link customer equity to business value, companies need to measure it. There are several methods for measuring customer equity, but the most widely used is Customer Lifetime Value (CLV). CLV calculates the total net profit a company expects to earn from a customer throughout their relationship with the business.

Steps to Measure Customer Lifetime Value (CLV)

Average Purchase Value: Start by calculating the average purchase value. This is done by dividing total revenue by the number of purchases over a specific period.

Purchase Frequency Rate: Calculate the purchase frequency rate. This is determined by dividing the total number of purchases by the number of customers during the same period.

Customer Value: Multiply the average purchase value by the purchase frequency rate to determine the customer value.

Customer Lifespan: Estimate the average customer lifespan, which is the length of time a customer remains active with your brand.

Customer Lifetime Value: Finally, calculate CLV by multiplying customer value by customer lifespan. This gives the estimated total profit a company expects from a single customer.

For example, if a customer spends $100 per purchase and makes ten purchases a year, their customer value is $1,000. If the customer remains loyal for five years, the total CLV is $5,000.

Other Metrics to Consider

While CLV is the most common way to measure customer equity, businesses should also consider other key performance indicators (KPIs) to gain a complete picture. Some other important metrics include:

Churn Rate: The percentage of customers who stop buying from the business.

Customer Retention Rate: The percentage of customers who continue buying from the company over time.

Customer Satisfaction: This can be measured through surveys and feedback tools to determine how happy customers are with the company's products and services.

Strategies to Boost Customer Equity

Once a business has measured its customer equity, the next step is to implement strategies to increase it. Below are some key strategies that companies can use to boost customer equity and enhance their business value.

Improve Product Quality and Value: Value equity is rooted in how customers perceive the worth of a product or service. To enhance customer equity, businesses must continually improve the quality of their offerings. This means investing in product development, innovation, and customer feedback loops to ensure the products meet or exceed customer expectations.

Enhance Brand Perception: Brand equity plays a critical role in customer loyalty. Companies need to consistently deliver on their brand promise. Building a strong brand requires clear messaging, excellent customer service, and consistent customer experiences across all touchpoints. Successful brands build emotional connections with their customers, which fosters loyalty and increases customer equity.

Focus on Customer Retention: Retention equity is driven by a customer's likelihood to continue purchasing from the company. Businesses should focus on building long-term relationships with their customers. This can be achieved through personalized experiences, loyalty programs, and consistent follow-up. Engaging customers through email marketing, social media, and targeted offers helps keep the relationship strong and ensures that customers remain loyal.

Utilize Data and AI: Data-driven marketing and AI tools can help businesses better understand customer behaviors and preferences. AI can analyze customer data to predict future trends, identify the most valuable customer segments, and tailor personalized marketing campaigns. By leveraging data analytics, businesses can make informed decisions that improve customer experiences and boost customer equity.

Customer-Centric Innovation: Companies that innovate based on customer needs are more likely to increase customer equity. By listening to customers and using their feedback to develop new products or services, businesses can stay relevant in a fast-paced market. This keeps customers engaged and ensures they continue to see value in the brand.

The Connection Between Customer Equity and Financial Performance

Customer equity and financial performance are closely linked. As customer equity grows, so does the long-term value of the business. Loyal customers are more likely to spend more over time, refer new customers, and remain with the brand during economic downturns. These behaviors directly contribute to revenue growth.

Investors also pay attention to customer equity when evaluating a company. Companies with strong customer equity have predictable revenue streams and a loyal customer base, making them more attractive investments. As a result, businesses that invest in building and maintaining customer equity often see higher market valuations and stronger financial performance.

Linking customer equity to business value is not only about increasing profits — it's about creating a sustainable foundation for growth. By focusing on customer relationships, businesses can build a loyal customer base that provides ongoing value. This long-term approach leads to stronger financial performance, improved market position, and greater business success.

Measuring customer equity through metrics like CLV helps businesses make informed decisions and prioritize strategies that build loyalty and retention. By continually investing in customer value, brand perception, and customer retention, companies can enhance both their customer equity and overall business value.

CHAPTER 3

MANAGING YOUR BUSINESS THROUGH CUSTOMER EQUITY

In today's fast-evolving business landscape, customer-centric strategies are essential for sustained success. Companies that prioritize customer equity — the total value derived from a customer over the length of their relationship — are better equipped to thrive in competitive markets. Managing your business through customer equity means leveraging this approach to drive long-term growth, improve profitability, and enhance brand loyalty.

This chapter explores how businesses can use customer equity to guide their operations, the benefits of this approach, and strategies for making customer equity a core focus in daily business management.

The Importance of Customer Equity

Customer equity provides a clear indicator of the long-term health of a business. It is a more holistic measure than short-term metrics such as sales figures or quarterly profits. By focusing on customer equity, businesses can shift from a transactional mindset to a relationship-driven one, encouraging customer loyalty and maximizing lifetime value.

There are three key components that influence customer equity:

Value Equity: This refers to the customers' perception of a product or service's worth. It is influenced by factors such as quality, price, and convenience. Companies that continually deliver value build strong customer loyalty.

Brand Equity: Brand equity is the emotional connection customers have with a brand. It is shaped by experiences, marketing, and reputation. Businesses with strong brand equity create long-term bonds that transcend individual products.

Retention Equity: Retention equity measures a customer's likelihood of staying loyal to a company. By providing exceptional service and personalized experiences, businesses can boost retention and reduce churn.

These elements combine to create customer equity, offering a complete picture of the value customers bring over their lifetime.

How Customer Equity Drives Business Strategy

Managing a business through customer equity involves using this metric as a foundation for key decisions. By placing customer value at the center, businesses can create more sustainable and profitable operations.

Guiding Marketing and Sales Efforts

Customer equity helps businesses identify their most valuable customer segments. Instead of targeting every potential buyer, companies can focus their marketing resources on high-value customers who are likely to stay loyal and generate long-term profits.

Personalizing marketing campaigns based on customer lifetime value (CLV) data leads to higher conversion rates, better customer engagement, and stronger relationships.

For example, a business that identifies a segment of customers with high retention rates might allocate more resources to maintaining and growing that segment. Conversely, lower-value customer segments may require less investment or may be targeted with specific strategies to increase their value.

Shaping Product Development

Customer equity also informs product development decisions. By understanding what drives value for different customer segments, businesses can tailor their products and services to meet specific needs. Companies that listen to customer feedback and continuously innovate are better positioned to build products that strengthen customer loyalty.

For example, a tech company may analyze data from its highest-value customers to identify new features or upgrades that will improve their experience. Developing products with customer equity in mind ensures that businesses are not just creating solutions for the present but are investing in long-term satisfaction.

Enhancing Customer Experience

Customer equity is closely tied to the customer experience. Businesses that manage their operations through the lens of customer equity invest in enhancing every touchpoint of the customer journey. This includes delivering seamless interactions, providing exceptional customer support, and personalizing services based on individual preferences.

Customers who have positive experiences are more likely to remain loyal and continue providing value. Moreover, satisfied customers often become advocates for the brand, leading to new customer acquisition through word-of-mouth referrals.

Optimizing Resource Allocation

By focusing on customer equity, businesses can make smarter decisions about resource allocation. Instead of spreading resources thinly across all customer segments, companies can prioritize those that offer the highest potential for long-term profitability. This approach allows businesses to optimize their spending on marketing, product development, and customer service to maximize returns.

For example, a company may decide to allocate more budget to a customer loyalty program designed to retain high-value customers, knowing that retaining existing customers is often more cost-effective than acquiring new ones.

Strategies for Managing Business with Customer Equity

To successfully manage your business through customer equity, it's important to adopt strategies that foster customer loyalty and long-term value. Here are some practical approaches:

Implement Customer Segmentation

Customer segmentation allows businesses to divide their customer base into distinct groups based on demographics, behaviors, and purchase history. This segmentation helps in targeting high-value customers with personalized marketing messages, tailored product offerings, and loyalty incentives.

By focusing on the most valuable customer segments, businesses can improve customer retention and increase the likelihood of repeat purchases.

Measure and Track Customer Lifetime Value (CLV)

To manage customer equity effectively, businesses need to measure and track CLV. This metric calculates the total net profit a business can expect from a customer over the course of their relationship. By regularly analyzing CLV, companies can identify which customers are most profitable and adjust their strategies accordingly.

CLV also helps businesses predict future revenue, allowing them to make informed decisions about where to invest resources for maximum return.

Enhance Personalization through Data and AI

Personalization is key to improving customer loyalty and increasing customer equity. Businesses can use data analytics and AI to offer highly personalized experiences based on customer preferences, buying behaviors, and interaction history.

AI can analyze large volumes of data to identify trends and predict future customer needs. This allows businesses to anticipate customer desires and deliver tailored solutions that enhance satisfaction and loyalty.

Focus on Customer Retention Strategies

Customer retention is a major factor in customer equity. It's often more profitable to retain existing customers than to acquire new ones. To boost retention, businesses should focus on delivering consistent value, offering rewards programs, and maintaining excellent customer service.

Loyalty programs that reward repeat purchases or exclusive offers for long-term customers can help strengthen retention. Additionally, businesses should regularly gather feedback to address any customer pain points before they lead to churn.

Invest in Brand Building

Brand equity is an essential component of customer equity. Businesses should invest in building a strong brand that resonates with their target audience. This involves delivering on promises, creating consistent and memorable experiences, and maintaining a positive reputation.

A strong brand not only attracts new customers but also encourages existing ones to stay loyal. By fostering an emotional connection with the brand, businesses can increase customer lifetime value and drive long-term growth.

Challenges in Managing Through Customer Equity

While managing a business through customer equity offers numerous benefits, there are also challenges to consider. One major challenge is the complexity of gathering and analyzing customer data. Businesses need the right tools and systems in place to track customer behavior, measure CLV, and gain insights into customer preferences.

Additionally, balancing short-term profits with long-term customer equity can be difficult. In some cases, businesses may need to invest in improving customer experience or product development, which can impact immediate profitability but yield higher returns in the future.

Aligning all departments within a company to prioritize customer equity can also be a challenge. It requires a company-wide commitment to customer-centric practices and a shift in culture to view customers as long-term assets rather than short-term revenue sources.

Managing your business through customer equity is a powerful strategy for driving sustainable growth and long-term success.

By focusing on the lifetime value of your customers, businesses can make smarter decisions about marketing, product development, and customer service.

Prioritizing customer retention, enhancing personalization, and building strong brand equity are essential steps in increasing customer loyalty and maximizing customer equity. While there may be challenges in gathering data and balancing short-term profitability, the long-term rewards of a customer-centric approach are undeniable.

By continuously measuring and optimizing customer equity, businesses can create a loyal customer base that generates value for years to come.

CHAPTER 4

ARE YOU OVERLOOKING THE VALUE OF YOUR CUSTOMERS?

In the fast-paced world of business, it is easy to focus on numbers, sales targets, and quarterly reports. However, the true value of a company lies not only in its products, services, or profits but in the strength of its customer relationships.

Many companies, in their quest for growth and profitability, overlook the immense value their customers bring to the business. This chapter explores why customers are the most valuable asset for any organization and how businesses can stop underestimating their importance.

The Hidden Value of Customers

Customer Loyalty: Loyal customers provide consistent revenue over time. Unlike one-time buyers, loyal customers return for future purchases. Their continued business creates a reliable income stream, reducing the need for constant marketing efforts to acquire new customers. Furthermore, retaining existing customers is generally much more cost-effective than acquiring new ones.

Word-of-Mouth Marketing: Satisfied customers are one of the most powerful marketing tools. When customers have positive experiences with a brand, they often share these experiences with their friends, family, and colleagues. This form of marketing is highly trusted, often leading to new customer acquisition at little or no cost to the business.

A strong customer base can essentially become a team of brand ambassadors, advocating for the company in ways that traditional marketing can't.

Customer Feedback: Customers provide valuable feedback that can help improve products and services. They are the ones interacting with the brand on a day-to-day basis and can offer insights into what is working and what needs improvement.

Listening to customer feedback allows businesses to make necessary changes and enhance their offerings. Ignoring this feedback is like overlooking a treasure trove of information that could lead to increased satisfaction and loyalty.

Increased Customer Lifetime Value (CLV): Customers who stay with a company for a longer period contribute significantly to the business's bottom line.

By nurturing relationships and encouraging repeat purchases, businesses can increase the CLV, which represents the total revenue a customer generates throughout their engagement with the brand. The longer customers remain loyal, the higher their lifetime value.

Referrals and Reviews: In today's digital age, customer reviews can make or break a business. Positive reviews on platforms like Google, Yelp, or Amazon can drive new business by influencing other potential customers.

In contrast, negative reviews can deter prospects. Encouraging satisfied customers to leave reviews and refer others to your business can be a highly effective, low-cost strategy for growth.

Why Businesses Overlook Customer Value

Despite the clear benefits of customer loyalty and engagement, many businesses still underestimate their customers' value. This often happens for several reasons:

Short-Term Focus: Many companies focus on short-term gains like immediate sales or profit margins. This focus often leads businesses to prioritize customer acquisition over retention, failing to recognize that loyal customers contribute far more to long-term profitability. The pressure to meet quarterly targets can push businesses to ignore the bigger picture of building customer relationships.

Lack of Measurement: If a business does not track customer lifetime value (CLV) or customer retention metrics, it can easily overlook the long-term value that customers bring.

Many businesses focus solely on metrics like revenue or new customer acquisition, ignoring the importance of tracking customer retention, churn rate, and loyalty.

Overemphasis on Product: Some businesses focus so heavily on their product or service that they forget about the importance of customer experience. While a great product is essential, it alone is not enough to retain customers. How a business interacts with customers, responds to their needs, and resolves issues all play critical roles in customer satisfaction.

Failure to Engage: Some companies fail to actively engage with their customers beyond the initial sale. They do not follow up with their customers, ask for feedback, or offer additional value after the first transaction. This lack of engagement can lead to customer attrition and missed opportunities to strengthen customer loyalty.

How to Recognize and Maximize Customer Value

Businesses that recognize and actively invest in their customers can unlock new levels of growth and profitability. Below are some strategies to help companies recognize and maximize customer value.

Measure Customer Lifetime Value (CLV): One of the most important metrics for understanding customer value is CLV. Calculating CLV helps businesses determine the long-term profitability of each customer. To calculate CLV, multiply the average purchase value by the purchase frequency, and then multiply that result by the average customer lifespan. Tracking this number helps businesses identify which customers are worth investing more in.

For example, if a customer spends $1,000 per month, purchases three times a year, and stays loyal for five years, their CLV would be $15,000. Understanding this value allows businesses to allocate resources more effectively toward retaining these high-value customers.

Focus on Retention Over Acquisition: While attracting new customers is important, retaining existing ones should be a higher priority. Loyal customers are more valuable over time because they tend to spend more and are more likely to recommend the brand to others. Implementing a customer retention strategy can include loyalty programs, personalized marketing, and proactive customer service. Businesses should make a concerted effort to ensure customers feel valued at every stage of their relationship with the brand.

Actively Seek Feedback: Customer feedback is a goldmine of insights. Businesses should not only welcome feedback but actively seek it through surveys, reviews, or direct communication.

Understanding customer pain points and acting on their suggestions shows customers that their opinions are valued. This can lead to stronger relationships and increased loyalty.

Additionally, businesses should monitor online reviews and social media mentions to understand what customers are saying about their brand. Responding to both positive and negative reviews in a professional and timely manner can strengthen customer trust.

Personalize Customer Interactions: Today's customers expect personalized experiences. Businesses that leverage customer data to tailor their marketing messages, product recommendations, and communications are more likely to build long-term relationships.

Personalization can be as simple as addressing customers by their name in emails or offering product suggestions based on past purchases. Personalized marketing makes customers feel valued and understood, which can increase their loyalty and lifetime value.

Reward Loyalty: Loyalty programs are an excellent way to retain customers and encourage repeat purchases. Offering rewards such as discounts, exclusive offers, or points that can be redeemed for future purchases incentivizes customers to keep coming back.

These programs not only reward loyalty but also make customers feel appreciated, which strengthens their emotional connection to the brand.

Invest in Customer Experience: The customer experience is the cornerstone of customer value. From the ease of navigating a website to the quality of customer service, every interaction shapes how customers feel about a brand.

Businesses should invest in creating seamless, positive experiences across all channels, including in-person, online, and mobile.

Excellent customer service is particularly important. Companies that resolve issues quickly and efficiently build trust with their customers. This not only improves satisfaction but also increases the likelihood of repeat business.

Are you overlooking the value of your customers? If so, it's time to shift your focus. Customers are the most valuable asset a business has. Beyond their immediate purchases, they bring long-term revenue, loyalty, and advocacy.

By recognizing the full value of your customers and investing in building strong relationships, businesses can create a foundation for sustained growth. Measuring customer lifetime value, focusing on retention, and delivering personalized experiences are key strategies for unlocking this hidden value.

CHAPTER 5

LEVERAGING AI TO STRENGTHEN CUSTOMER RELATIONSHIPS

Artificial intelligence (AI) is transforming the way businesses interact with their customers. In a world where personalization and efficiency are key, AI offers tools that can help companies better understand their customers and provide tailored experiences. The ability to leverage AI to strengthen customer relationships is becoming a major competitive advantage in nearly every industry.

This chapter explores how businesses can use AI to build stronger, more meaningful relationships with their customers. We will look at how AI can enhance personalization, improve customer support, predict customer needs, and boost overall customer satisfaction.

Why AI Matters for Customer Relationships

Customer relationships are the cornerstone of business success. In the digital age, customers expect fast, personalized, and seamless interactions. Companies that fail to meet these expectations risk losing customers to competitors. This is where AI comes into play.

AI enables businesses to process large amounts of customer data, analyze behavior, and make predictions that allow for more personalized and effective interactions. By leveraging AI, companies can improve the overall customer experience and build lasting relationships that drive loyalty and retention.

Enhancing Personalization with AI

Personalization: AI allows companies to offer highly personalized experiences at scale. Gone are the days when businesses could rely on generic messages or offers. Customers now expect brands to understand their preferences, purchase history, and behavior.

AI-driven algorithms can analyze a customer's previous interactions, purchase patterns, and even online behavior to predict what they might want next. For example, e-commerce platforms like Amazon use AI to recommend products based on browsing history, previous purchases, and items viewed by similar customers.

This level of personalization can significantly increase customer satisfaction and boost sales.

Dynamic Content Personalization: Another way AI helps personalize customer experiences is through dynamic content. AI can adjust website content, emails, and even product offerings based on individual customer preferences in real-time. For instance, a clothing retailer might use AI to show a returning customer new items in their preferred style or size, making the shopping experience more engaging and relevant.

Predictive Analytics for Personalization: AI-driven predictive analytics allows companies to anticipate customer needs before they even arise.

By analyzing past data, AI can forecast future behaviors and preferences, enabling businesses to tailor offers and messages at the right time. For example, an AI tool could predict when a customer is likely to reorder a consumable product, prompting the business to send a timely reminder or discount offer.

Improving Customer Support with AI

Chatbots: AI-powered chatbots have revolutionized customer support. These intelligent tools can handle basic inquiries, provide instant responses, and assist customers 24/7. By answering common questions, chatbots free up human agents to handle more complex issues.

Chatbots also help businesses respond to customers instantly, reducing wait times and improving the overall customer experience.

For example, banks use AI chatbots to assist customers with balance inquiries, bill payments, and even fraud alerts. These bots use natural language processing (NLP) to understand and respond to customer questions, offering smooth and efficient interaction.

This not only enhances customer satisfaction but also reduces operational costs for the business.

AI for Ticket Routing: AI can also be used to streamline customer service operations through smart ticket routing. When a customer submits a query or request, AI can analyze the content and direct it to the most appropriate department or agent, reducing response time.

This ensures that issues are resolved quickly and by the right person, leading to a more positive customer experience.

Sentiment Analysis for Better Service: Sentiment analysis, powered by AI, helps businesses understand how customers feel about their interactions. AI can analyze text from customer reviews, support tickets, or social media posts to gauge whether the customer is happy, frustrated, or dissatisfied.

This allows businesses to intervene promptly if negative sentiment is detected and provide a solution before the issue escalates.

Predicting Customer Needs with AI

AI excels at making predictions based on data. By analyzing past behaviors, AI can help businesses anticipate what customers might need or want next. This proactive approach can dramatically improve customer satisfaction, as businesses can offer solutions before customers even ask for them.

Predictive Customer Service: AI can predict when a customer might encounter a problem with a product or service. For example, a telecom company could use AI to predict when a customer's data usage is about to exceed their plan limit and offer an upgrade before the customer experiences slow speeds or additional charges.

This proactive customer service not only prevents issues but also strengthens the relationship by showing that the company cares about its customers' needs.

Anticipating Purchase Behavior: AI can also predict when customers are likely to make a purchase or churn. By analyzing patterns in customer activity, such as a decrease in engagement or a change in buying habits, AI can alert businesses to intervene with targeted offers, discounts, or personalized messages to retain the customer.

This kind of predictive engagement ensures that businesses are one step ahead in nurturing their customer relationships.

Boosting Customer Satisfaction with AI

AI plays a vital role in improving overall customer satisfaction by making interactions more efficient and personalized. Satisfied customers are more likely to stay loyal to a brand, recommend it to others, and spend more over time.

Faster Problem Resolution: Customers expect quick resolutions to their problems. AI can speed up this process by providing instant solutions through chatbots or AI-powered self-service platforms.

When customers can quickly find answers to their questions or resolve issues on their own, they are more likely to have a positive experience with the brand.

AI-Powered Feedback Loops: AI helps businesses collect and analyze customer feedback in real-time. By analyzing customer reviews, surveys, and social media posts, AI can identify areas where the business is excelling and areas that need improvement.

This continuous feedback loop allows companies to make adjustments that directly impact customer satisfaction.

Hyper-Personalized Offers: AI enables businesses to create hyper-personalized offers that speak directly to a customer's preferences. This level of customization makes customers feel valued and understood.

Whether it's through personalized discounts, targeted product recommendations, or customized loyalty rewards, these AI-driven efforts lead to happier and more loyal customers.

Building Trust with AI

While AI offers numerous benefits, trust is a critical factor in maintaining strong customer relationships. Businesses must ensure that AI is used ethically and transparently. Customers want to know how their data is being used and expect that it will be handled securely.

Transparency and Data Privacy: Customers are becoming more concerned about how their data is collected and used. Businesses should be transparent about their AI practices, explaining how data is collected, analyzed, and used to improve customer experiences.

Additionally, companies must adhere to data privacy regulations, such as GDPR, to protect customer information and build trust.

Human-AI Collaboration: Although AI is powerful, it's essential to strike the right balance between AI and human interaction.

Customers appreciate efficiency, but they also value human empathy when dealing with more complex or emotional issues.

AI should be used to enhance, not replace, human interactions. For example, an AI chatbot can handle basic queries, but when a customer has a more complex problem, they should be able to quickly escalate to a human agent.

Leveraging AI to strengthen customer relationships is no longer a future trend—it's a current necessity. AI provides the tools to enhance personalization, improve customer service, predict customer needs, and boost overall satisfaction. By using AI effectively, businesses can build stronger, more meaningful connections with their customers, leading to increased loyalty and long-term success.

However, the key to success with AI is ensuring that it is used ethically and in a way that complements human interactions. When done right, AI can help businesses foster deeper relationships with their customers, driving growth and competitive advantage.

In a world where customer expectations are constantly evolving, AI offers the power to not only meet those expectations but to exceed them.

CHAPTER 6

FUELING BUSINESS GROWTH WITH AI

Artificial intelligence (AI) is no longer a futuristic concept. It has become a powerful tool that businesses are leveraging to fuel growth, improve efficiency, and drive innovation. From automating routine tasks to delivering personalized customer experiences, AI offers companies numerous ways to optimize their operations and unlock new opportunities for expansion.

This chapter explores how AI can be used to accelerate business growth, increase productivity, and create competitive advantages. We'll look at key applications of AI, how it transforms decision-making, and how companies can integrate AI into their growth strategies.

Why AI Is Essential for Business Growth

In today's digital age, businesses face an increasingly competitive market. Consumers expect fast, personalized services, and businesses must adapt to ever-changing market conditions. AI enables companies to respond to these challenges by automating processes, analyzing vast amounts of data, and predicting future trends. As a result, businesses can operate more efficiently, make smarter decisions, and deliver better customer experiences.

AI allows businesses to scale without necessarily adding more resources. This scalability is crucial for growth. By automating routine tasks, AI frees up human employees to focus on higher-value activities, such as strategy and innovation. Furthermore, AI provides real-time insights that help businesses identify growth opportunities and mitigate risks.

Automating Routine Processes for Efficiency

Task Automation: One of the most significant ways AI contributes to business growth is through task automation. Many repetitive and time-consuming tasks, such as data entry, reporting, and scheduling, can be fully automated with AI tools. This not only increases operational efficiency but also reduces the likelihood of human error.

For example, businesses use AI-powered automation to streamline customer service, manage supply chains, and process financial transactions. In the marketing realm, AI can automate email campaigns, social media posts, and ad targeting, ensuring that marketing efforts are both timely and relevant. By automating these tasks, businesses can focus on strategic initiatives that drive growth.

AI-Driven Operations Management: AI is also transforming operations management by enabling businesses to predict inventory needs, optimize production schedules, and improve logistics.

AI algorithms can analyze historical data and identify patterns that help businesses forecast demand with greater accuracy. This ensures that businesses maintain optimal inventory levels, reducing waste and minimizing costs.

For example, AI is used by retailers to predict seasonal demand, ensuring they have the right products in stock at the right time. By avoiding overstocking or stockouts, companies can improve cash flow and meet customer demands more effectively.

Enhancing Customer Experience with AI

Personalized Marketing: AI's ability to analyze data in real time is revolutionizing the way businesses interact with customers. Personalized marketing is one of the key drivers of business growth, and AI makes it possible to deliver highly targeted, relevant content to consumers. By analyzing customer behavior, preferences, and past interactions, AI can generate personalized product recommendations, tailored offers, and customized communication.

For instance, streaming services like Netflix and Spotify use AI to recommend shows, movies, and music based on a user's viewing or listening history. This level of personalization increases user engagement and satisfaction, which translates into long-term customer loyalty and retention.

AI-Powered Customer Support: AI also plays a vital role in enhancing customer service, which is critical for growth. AI-driven chatbots and virtual assistants provide 24/7 support, answering customer queries instantly and resolving issues more quickly. By offering immediate responses to common questions, AI improves the customer experience, leading to higher satisfaction levels.

For example, companies like Sephora and H&M use AI chatbots to assist customers with product inquiries, style advice, and online shopping, creating a seamless and enjoyable experience. This not only helps businesses retain customers but also reduces the workload on human support teams, allowing them to focus on more complex issues.

Predictive Customer Insights: AI helps businesses understand their customers on a deeper level by analyzing data to predict future behavior. With predictive analytics, businesses can anticipate customer needs, identify potential churn, and offer proactive solutions. This foresight allows businesses to maintain stronger relationships with their customers, boosting loyalty and driving repeat purchases.

Data-Driven Decision Making with AI

Faster and Smarter Decisions: AI enables companies to make data-driven decisions faster and more accurately. By processing large volumes of data in real-time, AI can identify trends, anomalies, and insights that would be difficult for humans to detect. This capability allows businesses to respond quickly to changes in the market, making informed decisions that fuel growth.

For example, AI is used in finance to analyze stock market data and predict price movements. Investors use AI to make rapid decisions based on real-time data, helping them to maximize returns and minimize risk. In retail, AI helps businesses adjust prices dynamically based on demand, competitor pricing, and inventory levels, optimizing profitability.

Reducing Decision Bias: One of the biggest challenges in decision-making is overcoming human biases. AI, when used correctly, can help reduce bias by relying solely on data to guide decisions.

This leads to more objective and accurate outcomes. In areas like hiring, AI can help identify the best candidates by focusing on skills and experience rather than subjective criteria, resulting in better hiring decisions that contribute to long-term business growth.

AI for Risk Management: AI is also transforming risk management by helping businesses identify and mitigate risks before they become major issues. For instance, AI can analyze patterns in financial transactions to detect fraudulent activity or assess potential risks in supply chains by monitoring global events. This proactive approach helps businesses minimize losses and protect their assets, which is crucial for sustained growth.

AI and Innovation

Driving Product Innovation: AI enables businesses to innovate faster by identifying gaps in the market and new product opportunities. By analyzing consumer trends, competitor activity, and emerging technologies, AI can help businesses develop new products and services that meet evolving customer needs.

For example, AI is heavily used in the pharmaceutical industry to speed up drug discovery. By analyzing vast datasets on chemical compounds and biological interactions, AI can identify potential new drugs in a fraction of the time it would take traditional methods. This kind of innovation opens up new revenue streams and helps businesses stay ahead of the competition.

Optimizing Research and Development (R&D): AI also enhances R&D efforts by enabling businesses to experiment more efficiently. AI can simulate different scenarios, test hypotheses, and predict outcomes, allowing businesses to refine their ideas and products before investing significant resources. This reduces the time and cost associated with bringing new products to market, accelerating growth and improving return on investment.

Scaling Businesses with AI

AI and Scalability: One of the greatest advantages of AI is its ability to scale with a business. As a company grows, its operations become more complex. AI helps manage this complexity by automating tasks, optimizing workflows, and providing insights that support growth.

Whether it's processing more customer data, managing larger inventories, or coordinating more complex supply chains, AI ensures that businesses can scale efficiently without sacrificing quality or performance.

AI in Human Resources (HR): AI can also scale HR operations by automating tasks such as resume screening, employee onboarding, and performance management. By reducing administrative tasks, HR teams can focus on talent development, employee engagement, and other initiatives that drive business growth.

For example, AI-powered HR tools like applicant tracking systems (ATS) can quickly sift through thousands of resumes, identifying the best candidates based on predefined criteria. This speeds up the hiring process, allowing businesses to scale their workforce more efficiently as they grow.

Integrating AI into Growth Strategies

AI as a Strategic Tool: To fuel business growth, companies must integrate AI into their overall strategy. AI should not be seen as a standalone tool but as an integral part of the business. This involves identifying areas where AI can add the most value, such as customer experience, marketing, operations, or decision-making, and aligning AI investments with broader business goals.

Building a Data-Driven Culture: Successful AI implementation requires a data-driven culture. Businesses must ensure that data is collected, analyzed, and shared across departments. Employees should be trained to understand how AI works and how to leverage it to improve performance. By fostering a culture that embraces AI and data, companies can unlock its full potential and drive growth.

Investing in AI Talent: As AI becomes more central to business operations, investing in AI talent is crucial. Businesses need skilled data scientists, AI engineers, and machine learning experts to develop, implement, and maintain AI solutions. Building a strong AI team ensures that businesses can continually innovate and adapt as the technology evolves.

AI is transforming the way businesses operate and grow. By automating processes, enhancing customer experiences, and enabling data-driven decisions, AI provides the tools needed for sustained business growth. However, success with AI requires a strategic approach—one that integrates AI into every aspect of the business, from operations to customer engagement.

As companies continue to harness the power of AI, they will be able to scale more efficiently, innovate faster, and build stronger relationships with their customers.

CHAPTER 7

AI AND SUBSCRIPTION MODELS: A NEW APPROACH

Subscription-based business models have gained immense popularity in recent years. Companies like Netflix, Spotify, and Amazon Prime have demonstrated how effective these models can be in creating steady revenue streams and fostering customer loyalty.

However, as competition grows and consumer expectations evolve, businesses need to find new ways to stay ahead. This is where artificial intelligence (AI) comes in. AI is revolutionizing subscription models, offering companies a new approach to optimizing their services, enhancing customer experiences, and driving growth.

This chapter explores how AI is transforming subscription-based business models, enabling companies to deliver more personalized experiences, improve customer retention, and predict future trends. We will also look at specific AI applications that can make subscription models more effective and profitable.

Why Subscription Models Thrive

Subscription models work because they offer value through convenience and predictability. Instead of relying on one-time purchases, companies can build long-term relationships with customers who pay a recurring fee in exchange for continuous access to services or products. This model not only ensures predictable revenue but also encourages customer loyalty over time.

However, the subscription economy is highly competitive. Customers can easily switch between services if they feel their needs are not being met. This is where AI steps in to help companies stay competitive by providing deeper insights into customer behavior and offering solutions that meet their individual preferences.

Personalizing the Subscription Experience with AI

Customized Recommendations: AI allows subscription services to deliver personalized content and product recommendations based on customer data. For example, streaming platforms like Netflix use AI algorithms to analyze users' viewing habits and recommend shows or movies that align with their preferences.

This level of personalization increases engagement and satisfaction, which in turn reduces churn.

AI-driven personalization also works in other subscription-based industries, such as e-commerce and digital media. For instance, beauty subscription boxes like Birchbox use AI to analyze customer profiles and preferences to curate personalized selections of products.

This personalized approach makes the subscription feel more tailored and valuable to the individual customer, enhancing their overall experience.

Dynamic Content Delivery: Another key advantage AI brings to subscription models is the ability to dynamically adjust content or product offerings in real-time. AI can monitor user behavior and preferences on an ongoing basis, making it possible to update recommendations or services as customer needs change. This creates a more responsive and adaptive experience for the user.

For example, Spotify uses AI to create personalized playlists based on a user's listening habits, such as "Discover Weekly" or "Daily Mix." These playlists are updated regularly, keeping users engaged with fresh content that feels customized just for them. By continuously adapting to the customer's tastes, AI helps subscription services maintain relevance and deepen the connection between the user and the brand.

Improving Customer Retention with AI

Predicting Churn: One of the biggest challenges subscription-based businesses face is customer churn, or the rate at which customers cancel their subscriptions. Retaining customers is crucial for maintaining a healthy subscription model. AI helps companies tackle this problem by predicting churn before it happens.

By analyzing customer behavior, such as login frequency, usage patterns, or declining engagement, AI can identify customers who are at risk of canceling their subscriptions. With this information, businesses can take proactive measures to retain these customers, such as offering personalized discounts, special incentives, or tailored content that re-engages their interest.

Personalized Retention Strategies: AI doesn't just predict churn—it also helps businesses develop targeted retention strategies. When AI detects that a customer is losing interest, the business can intervene with customized offers that are likely to resonate with that specific user.

For example, a streaming service might offer a customer a free month of premium content or a curated list of shows that align with their past viewing habits. This kind of personalized retention strategy can significantly reduce churn and keep customers engaged.

Optimizing Subscription Tiers: Subscription models often include multiple tiers, such as basic, premium, or family plans. AI helps businesses understand which customers are most likely to upgrade or downgrade their subscription levels. By analyzing user behavior, such as content consumption patterns or engagement with premium features, AI can identify users who are ready to move up to a higher tier.

For example, a fitness app might use AI to analyze which users consistently engage with advanced workout content, indicating that they may be willing to upgrade to a premium membership that offers additional resources. By targeting these users with well-timed promotions, businesses can increase their revenue and enhance the customer experience by offering the right plan at the right time.

AI-Powered Predictive Analytics in Subscription Models

Forecasting Demand: AI's predictive analytics capabilities help subscription-based businesses forecast demand more accurately. By analyzing historical data, current trends, and customer behavior, AI can predict future consumption patterns. This allows companies to plan inventory, adjust pricing, and scale services to meet customer needs without overextending resources.

For example, a meal kit delivery service like HelloFresh might use AI to predict how many customers will order specific meals in the coming weeks, allowing them to manage inventory efficiently and reduce food waste. Similarly, streaming platforms can use predictive analytics to anticipate which shows or genres will be popular in the future, enabling them to invest in the right content.

Anticipating Customer Needs: AI helps businesses go beyond just understanding current customer preferences—it enables them to anticipate future needs. By analyzing patterns in customer data, AI can predict when a customer may want to try a new product, service, or feature.

For instance, a news subscription service might use AI to predict when a user will be interested in specific types of articles or topics based on past reading habits.

With this knowledge, the service can proactively recommend relevant content, keeping users engaged and satisfied. This ability to anticipate and meet customer needs strengthens the relationship between the user and the brand, ultimately driving loyalty.

Dynamic Pricing and AI

Optimizing Subscription Pricing: AI can also help businesses optimize their subscription pricing. Dynamic pricing, powered by AI, allows companies to adjust prices in real-time based on factors such as demand, customer preferences, and market trends. This ensures that businesses remain competitive while maximizing revenue.

For example, a subscription service for digital products might use AI to determine the optimal price point for different customer segments. High-demand users might be willing to pay more for exclusive access or premium features, while price-sensitive customers could be offered discounts to encourage them to subscribe.

This flexible pricing strategy helps businesses attract a diverse range of customers while maintaining profitability.

Personalized Pricing Offers: AI can also personalize pricing offers for individual customers. Based on a customer's behavior, engagement, and payment history, AI can create personalized discount offers or pricing plans.

For instance, a company might offer a loyal customer a discount on an annual subscription renewal or provide a new customer with a limited-time promotional rate to encourage sign-ups.

Personalized pricing ensures that businesses maximize conversions and retain customers by offering pricing that feels tailored to their needs and preferences.

AI-Driven Insights for Business Growth

Data-Driven Decision Making: AI provides businesses with valuable insights that can drive long-term growth. By analyzing customer data, businesses can identify trends, preferences, and opportunities for improvement.

These insights can inform product development, marketing strategies, and service enhancements, ensuring that the business evolves in line with customer expectations.

For example, AI might reveal that a large portion of a subscription service's user base is interested in specific content or features. Armed with this information, the business can invest in developing these offerings further, creating additional value for customers and increasing satisfaction.

Identifying New Markets: AI can also help subscription-based businesses identify new market opportunities. By analyzing geographic, demographic, and behavioral data, AI can reveal potential customer segments that are underrepresented.

This allows companies to expand into new regions or target untapped customer groups with tailored marketing efforts.

For instance, a digital learning platform might use AI to identify areas where demand for online education is growing. This insight allows the company to invest in content development, marketing, and partnerships in those regions, fueling business growth.

AI is transforming the subscription business model by offering a new approach to customer engagement, retention, and personalization. Through predictive analytics, dynamic pricing, and personalized experiences, AI helps businesses create value for customers while driving long-term growth.

As competition in the subscription economy intensifies, companies that leverage AI will gain a significant competitive edge.

By anticipating customer needs, reducing churn, and optimizing pricing strategies, AI allows businesses to deliver more tailored, responsive, and efficient services. This not only enhances customer satisfaction but also ensures the business remains scalable and profitable in the long run.

Incorporating AI into subscription models is no longer just an option—it's a necessity for businesses looking to thrive in the digital economy.

CHAPTER 8

TOOLS AND STRATEGIES FOR CUSTOMER ACQUISITION

Customer acquisition is the foundation of business growth. Every successful company, regardless of industry, relies on a steady stream of new customers to thrive. But in today's competitive market, acquiring customers isn't as simple as it once was.

The rise of digital channels, changing consumer behaviors, and advancements in technology have transformed the customer acquisition landscape. To stay ahead, businesses must employ modern tools and strategies that not only attract new customers but also keep them engaged and loyal over time.

In this chapter, we will explore the most effective tools and strategies for customer acquisition. We'll cover everything from digital marketing and content creation to the use of AI and automation.

The goal is to help businesses design a comprehensive acquisition strategy that targets the right customers, reduces costs, and increases long-term value.

The Changing Landscape of Customer Acquisition

The customer acquisition process has evolved significantly over the past decade. Traditional methods, like cold calling or mass advertising, are no longer as effective as they used to be. Today, customers have more control over their buying journeys. They research online, compare prices, read reviews, and seek recommendations before making a purchase decision.

To succeed in this environment, businesses need to understand the modern customer journey and use data-driven strategies to attract and engage potential customers. This is where technology plays a crucial role. Digital tools and platforms enable companies to reach specific audiences, track behavior, and optimize campaigns for better results.

Key Tools for Customer Acquisition

Search Engine Optimization (SEO): SEO is a long-term strategy that helps businesses attract customers by improving their visibility on search engines like Google.

By optimizing website content, keywords, and technical elements, businesses can rank higher in search engine results pages (SERPs). This increases organic traffic and brings in more potential customers.

For example, a business that sells fitness equipment could use SEO to rank for keywords like "best home workout equipment" or "affordable treadmills." When potential customers search for these terms, the company's website appears in the results, increasing the chances of conversion.

Paid Advertising (PPC): Pay-per-click (PPC) advertising is a popular tool for acquiring customers quickly. Platforms like Google Ads and social media channels like Facebook and Instagram allow businesses to run targeted ads based on user interests, behaviors, and demographics. Unlike SEO, which takes time to show results, PPC campaigns can generate immediate traffic.

One key benefit of PPC is that it allows businesses to control their budget and bid for specific keywords or audience segments. By targeting the right audience, companies can maximize their return on investment (ROI) and acquire new customers at a lower cost.

Social Media Marketing: Social media platforms are powerful tools for customer acquisition. With billions of users worldwide, platforms like Facebook, Instagram, LinkedIn, and Twitter offer businesses the ability to engage directly with potential customers. Social media allows companies to build brand awareness, share valuable content, and interact with followers in real-time.

Successful social media marketing involves creating engaging content that resonates with the target audience. This can include blog posts, videos, infographics, or user-generated content. Additionally, social media advertising lets businesses target specific audience segments with tailored messages, further improving acquisition efforts.

Content Marketing: Content marketing is a strategy that focuses on creating valuable, relevant content to attract and engage potential customers.

Rather than pushing direct sales messages, content marketing aims to provide useful information that solves customer problems or answers their questions.

For example, a company selling skincare products could publish blog posts about skincare routines, ingredient benefits, or seasonal skincare tips. By offering valuable insights, the company positions itself as an expert in the industry and builds trust with potential customers. Over time, this trust can lead to conversions and customer acquisition.

Email Marketing: Email marketing remains one of the most effective tools for acquiring and nurturing leads. By building an email list, businesses can send personalized messages directly to potential customers. Emails can include product recommendations, special offers, or educational content designed to move prospects through the sales funnel.

Personalization is key to email marketing success. Businesses should segment their email lists based on user behavior, demographics, and preferences. This ensures that the right message reaches the right audience, increasing the likelihood of conversion.

AI and Automation in Customer Acquisition

AI-Powered Customer Insights: Artificial intelligence (AI) is transforming customer acquisition by providing deeper insights into customer behavior. AI can analyze large datasets to identify patterns, preferences, and trends. This allows businesses to tailor their marketing efforts more effectively and reach the right audience with the right message.

For example, AI-powered tools like predictive analytics can help businesses anticipate customer needs. By analyzing past behavior, AI can predict which customers are most likely to make a purchase, allowing companies to target these individuals with personalized offers. This approach increases conversion rates and improves the efficiency of acquisition campaigns.

Marketing Automation: Marketing automation tools allow businesses to streamline their customer acquisition efforts by automating repetitive tasks like email marketing, lead scoring, and campaign management.

Platforms like HubSpot, Marketo, and ActiveCampaign offer automation features that nurture leads over time, ensuring that potential customers are engaged with relevant content throughout their buyer journey.

For instance, a business can set up an automated email sequence that sends follow-up messages to potential customers who have expressed interest in a product but haven't yet made a purchase. These emails can include product information, testimonials, or limited time offers to encourage conversion.

Chatbots and Conversational AI: AI-powered chatbots are becoming increasingly popular for customer acquisition. These tools can engage with website visitors in real-time, answering questions, providing product recommendations, or guiding users through the purchasing process.

Chatbots improve customer experience by offering instant responses, reducing the time customers spend waiting for support.

For example, a chatbot on an e-commerce website can greet visitors, ask about their preferences, and recommend products based on their responses.

By offering personalized assistance, chatbots help businesses capture leads and drive conversions.

Effective Strategies for Customer Acquisition

Know Your Audience: The most important step in customer acquisition is understanding your target audience. Businesses must know who their ideal customers are, what they need, and how they behave. This involves conducting market research, analyzing customer data, and creating detailed buyer personas.

Once a business understands its audience, it can create targeted marketing campaigns that resonate with potential customers. This approach ensures that marketing efforts are focused on attracting high-quality leads that are more likely to convert into paying customers. **Build a Strong Value Proposition:** A compelling value proposition is critical for customer acquisition.

This statement explains why a potential customer should choose your product or service over competitors. It highlights the unique benefits and solutions your business offers.

For example, if you run a subscription box service that delivers healthy snacks, your value proposition could be: "Convenient, nutritious snacks delivered to your door every month—perfect for busy professionals who want to eat well." This clearly communicates the benefits and differentiates the business from other snack providers.

Use Multi-Channel Strategies: Today's customers interact with brands across multiple channels, from social media and search engines to email and websites. A successful customer acquisition strategy requires a multi-channel approach, ensuring that businesses can engage potential customers wherever they are. For example, a company might use SEO to attract customers through organic search, social media marketing to engage with followers, and PPC advertising to drive targeted traffic. By using multiple channels, businesses can maximize their reach and increase the chances of acquiring new customers.

Test and Optimize Campaigns: Customer acquisition is an ongoing process that requires continuous testing and optimization. Businesses should regularly analyze their acquisition campaigns to determine what's working and what isn't. This involves tracking key metrics like conversion rates, cost per acquisition (CPA), and return on ad spend (ROAS).

By running A/B tests on landing pages, ads, and email content, businesses can identify the most effective strategies and refine their approach. This data-driven approach ensures that customer acquisition efforts are always improving, leading to better results over time.

Customer acquisition is a critical aspect of business growth, and the tools and strategies available today offer businesses unprecedented opportunities to attract new customers. By leveraging SEO, PPC, social media, content marketing, and AI-powered insights, companies can create targeted, data-driven campaigns that resonate with their audience.

To succeed in customer acquisition, businesses must stay agile, continuously test and optimize their strategies, and focus on delivering personalized, valuable experiences to their potential customers. With the right approach, businesses can not only attract new customers but also build long-lasting relationships that fuel long-term growth.

CHAPTER 9

AI-DRIVEN TACTICS FOR ACQUIRING CUSTOMERS

In today's highly competitive business landscape, customer acquisition has evolved dramatically. Traditional marketing methods, while still useful, are no longer enough to keep businesses ahead of the competition. Artificial intelligence (AI) has become a game-changer in customer acquisition strategies, offering more personalized, efficient, and data-driven approaches.

AI-driven tactics provide businesses with the ability to target the right customers, optimize marketing campaigns, and automate various parts of the acquisition process. By leveraging AI, companies can increase their reach, reduce costs, and enhance the customer journey from the very first touchpoint. This chapter explores how AI can be used to revolutionize customer acquisition and the key tactics businesses can implement to drive growth.

Why AI is Essential for Customer Acquisition

AI has transformed the way businesses interact with potential customers. Through advanced algorithms and data analysis, AI can process vast amounts of information quickly and accurately. It helps companies make smarter, data-driven decisions, predicting customer behavior and identifying opportunities that would otherwise be missed.

One of the biggest advantages AI offers is its ability to personalize the customer experience. Today's consumers expect personalized content, recommendations, and offers. AI allows businesses to meet these expectations by analyzing customer data and creating tailored experiences that attract new customers and keep them engaged.

Moreover, AI can automate many aspects of the customer acquisition process, saving businesses time and resources. Whether it's automating marketing campaigns, analyzing customer data, or improving ad targeting, AI can significantly enhance the efficiency and effectiveness of customer acquisition efforts.

Key AI-Driven Tactics for Customer Acquisition

1. Predictive Analytics for Targeting

What it is: Predictive analytics uses AI to analyze historical data and predict future outcomes. In customer acquisition, this means analyzing past behaviors, preferences, and engagement patterns to forecast which prospects are most likely to convert into customers.

How it works: AI tools analyze large sets of customer data to identify patterns. This might include data from website visits, email engagement, social media interactions, and purchase history. By understanding these patterns, AI can predict which potential customers are most likely to respond to a marketing campaign or purchase a product.

Benefits: Predictive analytics allows businesses to focus their marketing efforts on high-value prospects, improving conversion rates and reducing acquisition costs. It also helps businesses anticipate customer needs, making it easier to deliver the right message at the right time.

2. AI-Powered Ad Targeting

What it is: AI-powered ad targeting allows businesses to reach the right audience with greater precision. By analyzing customer data and behavior, AI can optimize ad campaigns in real time to ensure they are shown to the people most likely to engage.

How it works: AI tools analyze data from various sources, such as social media platforms, search engines, and browsing behavior. This data is then used to create highly targeted ad campaigns. For example, AI can determine which demographic groups are more likely to respond to a particular ad and adjust targeting parameters accordingly.

Benefits: AI-powered ad targeting increases the efficiency of marketing spend by reducing waste on irrelevant audiences. It also improves the effectiveness of campaigns by delivering ads that resonate with the target audience. This leads to higher click-through rates (CTR) and conversion rates.

3. Personalization at Scale

What it is: Personalization at scale refers to the use of AI to deliver highly personalized customer experiences on a large scale. This includes personalized email campaigns, product recommendations, and content tailored to individual customer preferences.

How it works: AI analyzes customer data such as browsing history, purchase behavior, and social media activity to deliver personalized content. For example, an e-commerce platform might use AI to recommend products based on a customer's previous purchases or browsing behavior.

Benefits: Personalization increases engagement and customer satisfaction. When customers feel like a business understands their needs and preferences, they are more likely to engage with the brand and make a purchase. AI enables businesses to personalize content for thousands or even millions of customers, creating a more effective and scalable acquisition strategy.

4. Chatbots and Conversational AI

What it is: AI-powered chatbots and conversational AI provide real-time customer support and engagement. These tools can answer questions, guide customers through the buying process, and offer product recommendations, all without the need for human intervention.

How it works: Chatbots use natural language processing (NLP) to understand and respond to customer inquiries. They can be programmed to handle common customer questions, provide information about products, or assist with checkout.

Conversational AI can also engage customers in personalized discussions, helping businesses collect data and drive conversions.

Benefits: Chatbots and conversational AI improve the customer experience by providing instant responses and 24/7 support. This helps businesses engage with potential customers at any time, improving lead generation and conversion rates. Additionally, chatbots can capture valuable customer data during interactions, further refining marketing and acquisition strategies.

5. AI-Driven Content Creation

What it is: AI-driven content creation involves the use of AI tools to generate personalized and relevant content for marketing campaigns. This can include blog posts, social media updates, email copy, and even video scripts.

How it works: AI tools like natural language generation (NLG) analyze data to create content that is relevant to the target audience. For example, AI can write personalized email subject lines or generate blog posts based on trending topics in the industry. These tools can also suggest content ideas based on customer behavior and interests.

Benefits: AI-driven content creation saves time and resources by automating parts of the content production process. It also ensures that content is tailored to the target audience, increasing engagement and helping businesses attract new customers. Furthermore, AI can analyze the performance of content, allowing businesses to continuously optimize their marketing efforts.

6. Sentiment Analysis for Customer Insights

What it is: Sentiment analysis is an AI-driven tool that analyzes customer feedback, reviews, and social media comments to understand how customers feel about a brand or product.

How it works: AI algorithms scan text data from various sources, such as customer reviews, social media posts, and emails. These algorithms identify the sentiment behind the text—whether it's positive, negative, or neutral—and provide insights into customer opinions and preferences.

Benefits: Sentiment analysis helps businesses understand how customers perceive their brand. By analyzing feedback in real time, businesses can quickly identify potential issues and respond proactively. This not only improves customer satisfaction but also helps businesses fine-tune their acquisition strategies by focusing on what resonates with customers.

Using AI to Optimize the Customer Journey

AI is particularly valuable in optimizing the customer journey, from the first interaction to final conversion. By analyzing customer behavior at every stage, AI helps businesses identify where prospects are dropping off and how to re-engage them.

Journey Mapping with AI: AI can map out the customer journey by tracking how prospects interact with a brand across multiple touchpoints. From social media engagement to website visits and email opens, AI provides a comprehensive view of the customer journey.

Identifying Bottlenecks: Once the customer journey is mapped, AI can identify where prospects are getting stuck or losing interest. For example, AI might reveal that many customers abandon their shopping carts after viewing shipping costs. Businesses can then take action to address these bottlenecks, such as offering free shipping promotions or simplifying the checkout process.

Optimizing Conversion Paths: AI helps businesses optimize the conversion path by analyzing data to determine which marketing channels and tactics are most effective at driving conversions.

With these insights, businesses can focus their efforts on the channels that provide the highest return on investment (ROI) and adjust their strategies accordingly.

AI-Powered Metrics and Analytics for Customer Acquisition

AI also plays a key role in measuring the success of customer acquisition campaigns. AI-powered analytics tools provide real-time insights into how campaigns are performing, making it easier for businesses to track progress and optimize their strategies.

Real-Time Campaign Monitoring: AI tools allow businesses to monitor the performance of their marketing campaigns in real time. This includes tracking key metrics like conversion rates, click-through rates, and cost per acquisition (CPA). By analyzing these metrics, businesses can make data-driven adjustments to improve campaign outcomes.

Predictive Campaign Analysis: AI can also predict the success of future campaigns by analyzing past performance data. This helps businesses plan more effective campaigns and allocate resources more efficiently.

AI is transforming the way businesses approach customer acquisition. With the ability to analyze data, predict customer behavior, and personalize experiences, AI-driven tactics are essential for any business looking to stay competitive in today's market.

By leveraging predictive analytics, AI-powered ad targeting, chatbots, and AI-driven content creation, businesses can improve the efficiency and effectiveness of their acquisition strategies.

Additionally, AI tools like sentiment analysis and journey mapping provide valuable insights that help businesses optimize every stage of the customer journey.

As AI technology continues to evolve, businesses that embrace these tools will gain a significant advantage in attracting and retaining customers, ultimately driving long-term growth and success.

CHAPTER 10

AI'S ROLE IN SHAPING INFLUENCER MARKETING

Influencer marketing has become one of the most effective strategies for businesses to reach and engage with their target audience. By collaborating with individuals who have large followings on social media, brands can tap into a trusted relationship between influencers and their followers.

But as influencer marketing has grown in popularity, so have the challenges of managing and optimizing these campaigns. This is where artificial intelligence (AI) comes into play.

AI is transforming the influencer marketing landscape by making it more data-driven, efficient, and personalized. From finding the right influencers to predicting campaign outcomes, AI is helping businesses improve their influencer marketing strategies and generate better results.

This chapter explores the many ways AI is shaping the future of influencer marketing and how brands can leverage AI to maximize their marketing efforts.

Why Influencer Marketing Needs AI

As influencer marketing has exploded in recent years, managing influencer relationships and campaigns has become increasingly complex. There are thousands of potential influencers to choose from, and finding the right one for your brand can be time-consuming.

Moreover, monitoring campaign performance, tracking engagement, and ensuring a return on investment (ROI) is difficult without the right tools.

AI helps simplify and streamline these processes. By using advanced algorithms and data analysis, AI can help brands make better decisions, optimize their strategies, and ensure they are working with the right influencers.

With AI, influencer marketing moves from being an art to becoming more of a science, allowing businesses to run campaigns that are more targeted, efficient, and measurable.

AI in Influencer Identification

Finding the Right Influencers: One of the most critical steps in influencer marketing is finding the right influencers who align with your brand values and resonate with your target audience. Traditionally, marketers would spend hours researching influencers manually, looking at follower counts, engagement rates, and content quality.

AI changes this by automating the process.

How it works: AI-driven platforms can analyze thousands of influencer profiles across different social media platforms in a matter of minutes. These tools consider multiple factors, including the influencer's niche, follower demographics, engagement metrics, and content relevance to the brand.

For example, AI tools can scan Instagram, YouTube, and TikTok for influencers who post content related to a specific industry or product, making the selection process faster and more precise.

Benefits: Using AI to identify influencers ensures that brands partner with influencers who genuinely connect with their target audience. This improves campaign effectiveness and reduces the risk of collaborating with influencers who may not deliver results. Moreover, AI tools can help avoid "fake influencers" who have inflated follower counts but lack genuine engagement.

Audience Analysis: AI can go beyond simply identifying influencers by analyzing their followers in detail. This ensures that brands not only find influencers with large followings but also those with followers who match the brand's ideal customer profile.

How it works: AI analyzes audience demographics, such as age, gender, location, and interests, to determine whether an influencer's followers are relevant to the brand. For example, a beauty brand targeting young women may use AI to find influencers whose followers are predominantly women aged 18-34 and interested in skincare products.

Benefits: Audience analysis through AI ensures that influencer campaigns reach the right people, improving the chances of engagement and conversion. It also prevents businesses from wasting resources on influencers whose followers may not be interested in the brand's offerings.

AI in Influencer Campaign Management

Content Optimization: AI helps brands and influencers optimize content for better performance. AI-driven tools can analyze past content to identify which types of posts, captions, or formats generate the most engagement and conversions.

How it works: AI tools can scan an influencer's past posts and compare engagement metrics such as likes, comments, shares, and click-through rates. Based on this analysis, AI provides recommendations on how to structure future posts to maximize impact.

For instance, AI may suggest using specific keywords, hashtags, or image styles that have previously performed well with the influencer's audience.

Benefits: By optimizing content with AI, brands can increase the chances of their influencer campaigns resonating with audiences, leading to higher engagement rates and better overall campaign performance. AI ensures that the content is not only aligned with the influencer's style but also optimized to drive results.

Predicting Campaign Outcomes: AI can predict the potential outcomes of an influencer marketing campaign before it even begins. By analyzing historical data and trends, AI tools can forecast key metrics such as engagement rates, audience reach, and ROI.

How it works: AI algorithms analyze similar past campaigns, influencer performance, and audience behavior to provide insights into how well a campaign is likely to perform. This allows brands to set realistic goals and expectations for the campaign. For example, AI might predict that partnering with a particular influencer will lead to a 10% increase in website traffic or a specific number of conversions based on past results.

Benefits: Predictive analytics allow brands to make data-driven decisions, reducing the uncertainty involved in influencer marketing. Knowing potential outcomes in advance helps brands allocate their budgets more effectively and ensures that they are investing in influencers who are likely to deliver the best results.

AI in Campaign Measurement and ROI Tracking

Real-Time Performance Monitoring: AI allows brands to monitor influencer campaigns in real time, tracking key performance indicators (KPIs) such as engagement rates, clicks, conversions, and brand mentions. This level of monitoring ensures that brands can make adjustments to their campaigns as needed to optimize results.

How it works: AI tools can automatically track social media posts, analyze engagement, and provide reports on how well the campaign is performing. For example, if an influencer's post isn't generating the expected engagement, AI can flag this early on, allowing the brand to adjust its approach, whether that means changing the content or shifting the focus to another influencer.

Benefits: Real-time monitoring helps brands optimize campaigns while they are still running, ensuring that potential issues are addressed quickly. It also provides actionable insights that can be used to improve future campaigns, making influencer marketing efforts more efficient and effective.

Measuring ROI: One of the biggest challenges in influencer marketing is measuring the return on investment (ROI). AI simplifies this process by providing clear metrics on the impact of each campaign and influencer.

How it works: AI tracks metrics such as conversion rates, website traffic, sales, and brand sentiment to calculate the ROI of an influencer marketing campaign. For example, AI can attribute sales directly to influencer posts by tracking referral links, discount codes, or UTM parameters.

Benefits: Measuring ROI with AI ensures that brands have a clear understanding of which influencers and campaigns deliver the best results. This data can be used to refine future marketing efforts, ensuring that budgets are spent on influencers and strategies that provide the highest return.

AI in Fraud Detection and Brand Safety

Detecting Fake Followers and Engagement: One of the biggest risks in influencer marketing is partnering with influencers who have fake followers or artificially inflated engagement metrics. AI can help detect these fraudulent activities.

How it works: AI tools analyze patterns in engagement, such as sudden spikes in follower counts or abnormal engagement ratios. They can also detect bot activity or suspicious behavior that indicates an influencer may have purchased followers or likes.

Benefits: AI protects brands from wasting their budgets on influencers who do not have a genuine following. This ensures that influencer marketing campaigns reach real, engaged audiences, improving the overall effectiveness and integrity of the campaign.

Ensuring Brand Safety: AI can also help brands ensure that influencers align with their values and maintain a positive reputation. AI tools scan influencer content for any inappropriate or controversial material that could harm the brand's image.

How it works: AI analyzes past posts, comments, and interactions to identify potential red flags, such as offensive language, political opinions, or controversial content. This helps brands avoid working with influencers whose content may not align with their brand values.

Benefits: By ensuring brand safety, AI allows businesses to protect their reputation and avoid partnerships that could lead to negative publicity. This helps maintain trust with their audience and ensures that influencer collaborations are consistent with the brand's image.

AI is rapidly transforming the world of influencer marketing, making it more data-driven, efficient, and results-oriented. From identifying the right influencers to predicting campaign success and measuring ROI, AI-driven tools are helping businesses optimize their influencer marketing strategies.

By leveraging AI, brands can run more targeted campaigns, improve engagement, and ensure that their marketing efforts deliver measurable results. As AI technology continues to evolve, influencer marketing will become even more sophisticated, offering new opportunities for brands to connect with their audience in meaningful ways.

For businesses looking to succeed in influencer marketing, embracing AI is no longer an option—it's a necessity.

CHAPTER 11

DO CONSUMERS TRUST AI-DRIVEN INFLUENCERS?

One of the most intriguing developments is the rise of AI-driven influencers. These virtual personalities, created using AI and computer-generated imagery (CGI), have made a significant impact on social media platforms like Instagram, TikTok, and YouTube.

AI influencers, such as Lil Miquela, have millions of followers, engaging in campaigns for major brands. But with this new trend, an important question arises: Do consumers actually trust AI-driven influencers?

Trust is the cornerstone of influencer marketing. When followers feel a connection with an influencer, they are more likely to trust their recommendations, which leads to increased engagement and conversion rates.

This chapter explores whether AI-driven influencers can generate the same level of trust as their human counterparts and what factors influence consumer perceptions of these virtual personalities.

The Rise of AI-Driven Influencers

AI-driven influencers, also known as virtual or CGI influencers, are digital characters designed to look, act, and communicate like real people.

These influencers are often created by brands, creative agencies, or even independent designers using advanced AI algorithms, motion capture technology, and CGI. Their content is highly curated, and their "lives" are shaped to fit specific marketing goals.

Lil Miquela, for example, is one of the most well-known virtual influencers. She was created by a company called Brud and has worked with global brands like Calvin Klein, Prada, and Samsung.

AI influencers like Miquela have human-like features and personalities, and they interact with their followers in a way that mimics the engagement patterns of real human influencers.

The appeal of AI influencers lies in their control. Unlike human influencers, AI-driven influencers don't have personal scandals, unpredictable behavior, or the limitations of real life.

This control allows brands to craft and maintain a highly consistent, on-brand persona. But while these benefits are attractive to companies, the bigger question is whether consumers are willing to engage with—and trust—these digital personalities.

Trust in Influencer Marketing

Trust plays a crucial role in the effectiveness of influencer marketing. When an influencer recommends a product or service, followers tend to trust their opinions because they feel a personal connection.

Consumers perceive influencers as relatable figures who share their tastes, values, and lifestyle. This connection leads to a higher level of trust than they may have with traditional advertisements.

But when it comes to AI-driven influencers, the trust equation changes. Unlike human influencers, AI influencers lack the authenticity that comes from lived experiences.

Virtual influencers do not have personal stories, real emotions, or genuine struggles. These missing elements can affect how consumers perceive their credibility and trustworthiness.

Do Consumers Trust AI-Driven Influencers?

The answer to whether consumers trust AI-driven influencers is complex. While some consumers are open to the idea, others are skeptical. Several factors influence how consumers perceive and trust AI influencers.

1. Authenticity vs. Artificiality

Authenticity is one of the main reasons consumers trust influencers. People value influencers who are genuine, transparent, and relatable. AI-driven influencers, by their nature, are not real. They cannot provide personal experiences, human emotions, or true-life narratives. For many consumers, this artificiality can be a barrier to trust.

How it affects trust: While AI influencers can be programmed to appear authentic, many consumers find it difficult to relate to a digital entity.

The absence of real-life experiences can make AI influencers seem more like corporate marketing tools than trusted sources of information. This perception can reduce the level of trust consumers place in AI-driven influencers compared to human influencers.

2. Transparency and Disclosure

One of the most critical factors in building trust with consumers is transparency. In influencer marketing, followers expect to know when content is sponsored or when influencers are being paid to promote products.

With AI-driven influencers, transparency becomes even more important. Consumers want to know whether they are engaging with a real person or a digital creation.

How it affects trust: If consumers are fully aware that they are interacting with an AI influencer, and the brand is transparent about the influencer's virtual nature, it can foster a level of trust. However, if brands or creators attempt to conceal the fact that an influencer is AI-driven, it can lead to distrust and damage the brand's reputation. Clear disclosure is essential for maintaining trust in AI-driven influencer marketing.

3. Consistency and Reliability

AI-driven influencers can offer a high degree of consistency and reliability. Because they are programmed, they can maintain a constant voice, personality, and brand alignment.

They don't experience the same risks as human influencers, such as personal scandals, burnout, or fluctuations in behavior.

How it affects trust: For brands, this consistency can be a significant advantage. AI influencers will always deliver the same message and are unlikely to stray from their brand's core values.

This reliability may help build trust with certain consumers who appreciate consistency in the influencers they follow. However, the lack of human unpredictability may also make AI influencers seem less relatable and more "robotic," which could hinder trust among other consumers.

4. Engagement and Interaction

One of the key strengths of influencer marketing is the ability of influencers to engage with their followers on a personal level. Human influencers often respond to comments, share their personal experiences, and build a community around their content. AI-driven influencers can engage with followers, but the nature of that engagement is artificial and pre-programmed.

How it affects trust: For some consumers, the ability to engage with an AI influencer might be enough to foster a sense of connection. If the AI influencer interacts consistently and thoughtfully, followers might develop a relationship similar to the one they have with human influencers.

However, for others, knowing that the responses are not genuine or come from an algorithm may diminish the sense of trust and authenticity.

Generational Differences in Trust

Another factor to consider is how different generations view AI-driven influencers. Younger consumers, particularly Gen Z, are often more accepting of AI technology and virtual worlds. This generation has grown up in a digital-first environment and may be more open to interacting with AI influencers, especially if they view them as part of a larger entertainment ecosystem.

In contrast, older generations, such as Millennials and Gen X, may be more skeptical of AI-driven influencers. These consumers often value human connection and authenticity more highly and may have difficulty trusting an influencer that they know is not real.

The Future of AI-Driven Influencers

As AI technology continues to improve, AI-driven influencers will likely become even more sophisticated. Advances in natural language processing (NLP), emotion detection, and machine learning could make AI influencers seem more human, blurring the line between virtual and real personalities.

In the future, AI influencers may be able to engage with followers in ways that feel more authentic, using data-driven insights to personalize interactions on a deeper level. However, brands will need to remain transparent about the nature of AI influencers to maintain trust.

How Brands Can Build Trust with AI-Driven Influencers

For brands looking to use AI-driven influencers in their marketing strategies, building trust is key. Here are a few ways to ensure that AI influencer campaigns resonate with consumers:

Transparency: Be upfront about the fact that the influencer is AI-driven. Transparency will prevent consumers from feeling deceived and can help foster a sense of openness.

Clear Value Proposition: Ensure that the AI influencer provides real value to the audience. Whether it's through entertainment, education, or product recommendations, the influencer should offer something meaningful to followers.

Personalization: Use AI to personalize content and engagement. By tailoring content to individual follower preferences, AI-driven influencers can create a more relevant and engaging experience.

Consistent Engagement: Ensure that the AI influencer engages with followers regularly and consistently. Responding to comments and interacting with followers can help build a sense of community, even if the influencer is virtual.

Do consumers trust AI-driven influencers? The answer depends on a variety of factors, including transparency, authenticity, and engagement.

While some consumers, particularly younger generations, are more open to interacting with virtual influencers, others may struggle to trust influencers they know are not real.

As AI technology continues to evolve, the role of AI-driven influencers in marketing will likely expand.

Brands that are transparent and thoughtful in their use of AI influencers can build trust and engagement with their audience, driving meaningful results in their marketing efforts.

CHAPTER 12

WILL AI REPLACE HUMAN CONTENT CREATORS?

The rise of artificial intelligence (AI) has transformed numerous industries, from healthcare to finance, and now it is making its way into the world of content creation. AI-powered tools are capable of writing articles, creating videos, designing graphics, and even generating social media posts. As these technologies become more sophisticated, a pressing question arises:

Will AI replace human content creators?

While AI's role in content creation is growing, the answer is not so straightforward. AI offers speed, scalability, and efficiency, but it lacks the creativity, emotion, and nuanced understanding that human creators bring to their work.

In this chapter, we will explore the capabilities of AI in content creation, its limitations, and how human creators and AI can complement each other.

The Capabilities of AI in Content Creation

AI has advanced to a point where it can produce content quickly and at scale. Through machine learning, natural language processing (NLP), and neural networks, AI systems can analyze data, understand language patterns, and generate written, visual, and audio content.

AI-Generated Writing: Tools like GPT-3 (the engine behind this text) can generate blog posts, product descriptions, and even news articles. These systems analyze massive amounts of data to understand language structures and predict what comes next in a sentence. They can write coherent and grammatically correct content on virtually any topic, often indistinguishable from what a human might write.

AI-Driven Design and Visual Content: AI can also generate images, graphics, and video content. Tools like Adobe Sensei use AI to automate aspects of graphic design, including photo editing and layout generation. AI can create digital art, enhance images, and even develop entire video sequences. Brands and marketers can use AI to produce visual content faster, allowing for quicker turnaround times on campaigns.

AI for Social Media Content: Social media platforms thrive on regular updates and timely content. AI tools like Lately.ai and Jarvis.ai can generate social media posts, suggest hashtags, and even determine the best times to post based on audience engagement data. AI can analyze which types of content resonate most with users and replicate similar formats to maintain audience interest.

Personalized Content at Scale: One of AI's greatest strengths in content creation is its ability to generate personalized content at scale.

For instance, AI can create thousands of personalized emails or product recommendations tailored to individual users, based on their browsing history and preferences.

Human content creators can't match this level of personalization at the same speed and volume, making AI a valuable tool for delivering customized experiences.

The Limitations of AI in Content Creation

While AI offers numerous advantages in terms of speed, scale, and efficiency, it has limitations that prevent it from fully replacing human content creators. Creativity, emotional depth, and cultural understanding are areas where AI falls short.

Lack of Originality and Creativity: AI excels at replicating patterns, but it struggles with true creativity. While AI can generate content that mimics human writing or design, it is often formulaic and lacks originality.

AI is trained on existing data, which means it can only produce content based on what it has already learned. Human creators, on the other hand, can break away from established norms, innovate, and bring fresh perspectives that AI cannot replicate.

For instance, a human writer can develop a unique narrative voice or create a story that challenges conventions, whereas AI-generated content often follows predictable structures. Similarly, a human designer can bring artistic flair, experimenting with new styles, while AI typically sticks to established design rules.

Emotional Depth and Storytelling: One of the key reasons people engage with content is the emotional connection it creates.

Whether it's a moving story, a humorous article, or an inspiring video, human content creators understand how to tap into emotions in a way that AI cannot.

AI-generated content lacks the emotional intelligence to craft meaningful narratives. It can write an article based on data, but it struggles to weave in the subtle emotions, cultural references, or deep storytelling techniques that human creators excel at. This emotional depth is what often makes content memorable, persuasive, and impactful.

Understanding Context and Nuance: AI can process large amounts of data, but it struggles with understanding context, especially in complex or sensitive situations. Human content creators have the ability to interpret cultural nuances, social dynamics, and ethical considerations that AI might miss.

For example, writing an article about a sensitive topic such as mental health requires a deep understanding of human psychology and empathy, which AI cannot replicate.

Additionally, AI can misinterpret slang, idiomatic expressions, or humor, leading to content that feels awkward or out of place. Human creators, with their deep understanding of language and context, are better equipped to produce content that resonates with diverse audiences.

Human-AI Collaboration in Content Creation

While AI may not fully replace human content creators, it is becoming an indispensable tool in content creation workflows. The real potential lies in the collaboration between human creativity and AI's efficiency.

When used together, AI can handle repetitive, data-driven tasks, while human creators focus on the more nuanced and creative aspects of content development.

AI as a Creative Assistant: AI can assist human creators by handling the "heavy lifting" of content creation. For example, a writer can use AI to generate a first draft or outline for an article, saving time on research and initial structuring.

The writer can then refine and enhance the content, adding personal insights, creative flair, and emotional depth that only a human can provide.

Similarly, AI tools can assist graphic designers by automating tedious tasks like resizing images, adjusting colors, or generating multiple variations of a design. This allows designers to focus on higher-level creative decisions, experimenting with new concepts and ideas.

Speeding Up Content Production: AI's ability to generate content quickly makes it a valuable tool for industries that require a high volume of content. For instance, news outlets and e-commerce platforms can use AI to produce real-time updates, product descriptions, or reports.

Human creators can then focus on more in-depth analysis, investigative reporting, or long-form content that requires critical thinking and original insights.

Enhancing Personalization: AI excels at data-driven personalization, allowing businesses to create customized experiences for each user.

Human creators can craft overarching strategies and brand message, while AI personalizes the content to individual preferences at scale.

For example, a marketing team can develop a campaign's creative vision, while AI generates personalized emails, product recommendations, or social media ads tailored to different segments of the audience.

The Future of AI in Content Creation

As AI technology continues to advance, its role in content creation will likely expand. AI may become better at understanding context, recognizing emotions, and even mimicking creativity. However, there will always be certain aspects of content creation that require the human touch.

AI as a Co-Creator: In the future, AI is likely to play an even greater role as a co-creator, helping human content creators push the boundaries of what is possible. AI could assist with brainstorming, generating multiple creative concepts that human creators can then refine. This partnership could lead to faster content production and more innovative ideas.

Ethical Considerations and Transparency: As AI's role in content creation grows, ethical considerations will become more important. Transparency is crucial audiences need to know when content has been created or influenced by AI.

Additionally, there are concerns about AI-generated misinformation or the devaluation of creative professions. Businesses and content creators will need to navigate these challenges carefully.

While AI is revolutionizing content creation, it is unlikely to fully replace human content creators. AI excels at tasks that involve data analysis, automation, and scalability, but it lacks the creativity, emotional intelligence, and nuanced understanding that humans bring to the table.

The future of content creation lies in collaboration. AI can handle repetitive tasks, speed up production, and enhance personalization, while human creators focus on crafting original, engaging, and emotionally resonant content.

By working together, AI and human creators can unlock new possibilities in the world of content, driving innovation and delivering more impactful experiences for audiences.

In the evolving world of content creation, AI will be a powerful tool, but human creativity will remain irreplaceable.

CHAPTER 13

EXPLORING THE POTENTIAL OF GENERATIVE AI

Generative AI is one of the most exciting and transformative advancements in artificial intelligence today. Unlike traditional AI models that perform specific tasks based on predefined rules or datasets, generative AI creates new content, whether it's text, images, music, or even entire videos. This technology has the potential to revolutionize industries ranging from marketing and design to healthcare and entertainment.

In this chapter, we'll explore what generative AI is, how it works, and the many ways it's shaping the future. We'll also dive into its capabilities, potential applications, and the ethical questions that arise as AI takes on more creative tasks.

What Is Generative AI?

Generative AI refers to a subset of AI systems designed to generate new content that mimics human creation. These AI models use deep learning techniques such as neural networks, which are trained on vast datasets to learn patterns, structures, and relationships within that data. After training, these models can generate new, original content that resembles the data they were trained on.

Popular generative AI tools, like OpenAI's GPT-3 for text generation or DALL·E for image creation, have demonstrated the incredible possibilities of this technology. From writing articles to designing virtual environments, generative AI pushes the boundaries of what machines can do creatively.

How Does Generative AI Work?

At its core, generative AI relies on machine learning models that use algorithms to identify patterns in data and produce similar outputs. The most common architecture for generative AI is a neural network called a **Generative Adversarial Network (GAN)**.

How GANs work: GANs consist of two networks: a **generator** and a **discriminator**. The generator creates new data samples, such as images or text, while the discriminator evaluates these samples to determine whether they are real or generated.

Through an iterative process, the generator improves its outputs to make them increasingly indistinguishable from real data, while the discriminator gets better at spotting fakes. This back-and-forth competition helps both models improve over time.

Other generative AI models, such as **Transformer-based models** (used in tools like GPT-3), rely on vast amounts of data and advanced algorithms to generate coherent, contextually relevant outputs.

These models predict the next word in a sentence or the next pixel in an image based on the patterns they've learned from their training data.

Applications of Generative AI

Generative AI's versatility has led to a wide range of applications across industries. Below are some of the most promising uses of this technology.

1. Content Creation

Generative AI is revolutionizing content creation by automating the production of written, visual, and audio content. In marketing, AI tools like Jasper and Copy.ai can generate blog posts, social media captions, and product descriptions at a scale. This not only saves time but also allows businesses to maintain a consistent content output.

Examples of content creation:

Text Generation: AI models like GPT-3 can generate news articles, fiction, or even technical reports. These models analyze existing content and create new pieces that mimic human writing styles.

Image Generation: Tools like DALL·E and MidJourney can create unique images from textual descriptions. For instance, a designer might input a phrase like "a futuristic cityscape at sunset," and the AI generates a visually striking image that matches the description.

2. Design and Creativity

In fields like architecture, fashion, and graphic design, generative AI can assist by producing creative concepts and prototypes. AI-generated designs can serve as inspiration for human creators or as a starting point for more refined work. Designers can input a few key parameters, and the AI generates multiple design options, allowing them to explore new ideas more efficiently.

Examples of creative AI:

Architectural design: AI can generate unique building layouts based on specific criteria such as sustainability, space efficiency, or aesthetic preferences.

Fashion design: AI tools like Glitch, DeepDream, and RunwayML help fashion designers create novel patterns, clothing styles, or fabric textures that push the boundaries of conventional design.

3. Healthcare

Generative AI is making inroads into healthcare by accelerating drug discovery, creating personalized treatment plans, and even generating synthetic medical data for research purposes. AI models can simulate thousands of potential drug compounds and their effects on diseases, significantly speeding up the process of drug development.

Examples in healthcare:

Drug discovery: Generative AI models analyze chemical structures and biological data to propose new molecules that might be effective treatments for specific conditions.

Medical imaging: AI tools can generate synthetic medical images to train healthcare professionals or improve the accuracy of diagnostics without relying on large sets of real patient data.

4. Entertainment and Media

Generative AI is being used to create everything from music and artwork to video games and movies. AI-generated music can compose original scores based on inputted genres or moods, while AI in gaming can design entire virtual worlds, including characters, landscapes, and narratives.

Examples in entertainment:

Music composition: AI tools like Amper and AIVA can compose original music for films, video games, or advertisements, based on specific parameters such as genre, tempo, and mood.

Video production: Generative AI can help automate the creation of video content, generating realistic visuals, animations, or special effects in films and games. It can even simulate actors or alter existing footage seamlessly.

Ethical Considerations of Generative AI

While the potential of generative AI is vast, its rise also brings several ethical challenges that need to be addressed.

1. Deepfakes and Misinformation

One of the most concerning uses of generative AI is the creation of deepfakes—realistic but fake videos or audio that can depict people saying or doing things they never actually did.

Deepfakes can be used to spread misinformation, manipulate public opinion, or cause personal and reputational harm.

Challenges with deepfakes: Deepfakes are particularly concerning in political contexts, where AI-generated content can mislead the public, create confusion, or even incite violence. Detecting and mitigating the harmful use of deepfakes remains a critical challenge for AI developers and policymakers.

2. Copyright and Ownership

Generative AI blurs the line between human creativity and machine-generated content, raising questions about copyright and intellectual property. If an AI generates an original artwork or piece of music, who owns the rights to it—the user, the creator of the AI model, or the AI itself?

Legal implications: As AI-generated content becomes more prevalent, new legal frameworks may need to be developed to determine how ownership and copyright are handled. This is particularly important for artists, writers, and other creators whose livelihoods could be affected by AI-generated works.

3. Bias and Fairness

Generative AI models are trained on large datasets, and if those datasets contain biased information, the AI can reproduce or even amplify these biases in the content it generates. For instance, AI might unintentionally reinforce gender or racial stereotypes in the content it creates.

Addressing bias: Developers need to ensure that the datasets used to train generative AI models are diverse and free from harmful biases. Additionally, ongoing monitoring and refinement of AI outputs are crucial to preventing the spread of biased or offensive content.

The Future of Generative AI

Generative AI is still in its early stages, and as the technology matures, we can expect even more sophisticated and impactful applications across industries. Advances in AI will likely make generated content increasingly indistinguishable from human-created work, further pushing the boundaries of what AI can accomplish.

More Human-Like Creativity: Future AI models will likely become better at mimicking human creativity, producing content that feels more emotionally resonant and contextually aware. This could open new possibilities in art, literature, and entertainment.

Collaboration Between AI and Humans: Rather than replacing human creators, generative AI is expected to enhance creativity by serving as a tool that complements human intuition and imagination. In fields like design, advertising, and media, AI will likely play a collaborative role, generating ideas and content that human creators can refine and build upon.

AI-Driven Innovation: Generative AI has the potential to drive innovation in unexpected ways. By exploring combinations of ideas or concepts that humans might not think of, AI could lead to breakthroughs in science, technology, and creative industries.

This could result in entirely new forms of media, art, and products that redefine what's possible.

Generative AI is a powerful technology that has the potential to reshape industries, from content creation to healthcare and beyond.

While it offers exciting possibilities for automating tasks, creating new art forms, and solving complex problems, it also raises important ethical and societal questions that must be carefully considered.

The future of generative AI will likely involve a collaborative relationship between humans and machines, where AI serves as a creative partner rather than a replacement for human ingenuity.

As this technology evolves, it will unlock new opportunities and challenge our understanding of creativity, authorship, and innovation.

CHAPTER 14

MERGING AI WITH CUSTOMER RETENTION EFFORTS

Customer retention is crucial to business success. Keeping existing customers is far more cost-effective than acquiring new ones, and loyal customers tend to spend more over time.

In today's competitive market, businesses are increasingly turning to artificial intelligence (AI) to enhance their customer retention strategies. AI allows companies to predict customer behavior, personalize experiences, and automate engagement, all of which can lead to higher retention rates.

This chapter explores how merging AI with customer retention efforts can help businesses build long-term relationships with their customers, reduce churn, and maximize lifetime value. We will also look at specific AI-driven tools and strategies that can improve retention efforts and keep customers engaged.

Why Customer Retention Matters

Before diving into how AI can enhance customer retention, it's important to understand why retention is a critical factor for business growth. Studies consistently show that it costs five to seven times more to acquire a new customer than to retain an existing one. Moreover, increasing customer retention by just 5% can boost profits by 25% to 95%, depending on the industry.

Loyal customers are also more likely to advocate for a brand, recommend it to others, and spend more over time. However, retaining customers is challenging, especially in a crowded marketplace where customers have endless options. This is where AI can make a significant impact.

How AI Enhances Customer Retention

AI provides businesses with the tools to better understand their customers, anticipate their needs, and engage them in meaningful ways. Below are several ways AI enhances customer retention efforts.

1. Predicting Customer Churn

What it is: Customer churn occurs when customers stop doing business with a company. AI-driven churn prediction models analyze data and identify customers who are likely to churn, enabling businesses to take proactive steps to retain them.

How it works: AI models analyze customer behavior, such as purchase frequency, engagement levels, browsing patterns, and transaction history, to detect early warning signs of churn. For example, if a customer's engagement drops significantly or if they stop using certain products or services, the AI model flags this customer as at-risk.

Benefits: By identifying at-risk customers early, businesses can implement targeted retention strategies, such as personalized offers, discounts, or engagement efforts, to re-engage them. AI enables companies to take a proactive approach rather than waiting until it's too late to intervene.

2. Personalizing Customer Engagement

What it is: Personalization is one of the most effective ways to keep customers engaged. AI-driven personalization uses data to create individualized experiences that make customers feel valued.

How it works: AI tools collect and analyze data from multiple touchpoints, including purchase history, browsing behavior, and customer feedback. This allows businesses to tailor communication, product recommendations, and promotions to each customer's unique preferences.

For example, an e-commerce company can use AI to recommend products based on past purchases or browsing history. A streaming service might suggest movies or shows based on a customer's viewing habits. These personalized experiences increase customer satisfaction and foster loyalty.

Benefits: Personalized engagement makes customers feel understood and valued, which strengthens their relationship with the brand. It also increases the likelihood of repeat purchases and long-term loyalty.

3. Automating Customer Support with AI

What it is: Customer support is a key aspect of retention. AI-driven tools like chatbots and virtual assistants provide instant, 24/7 support, improving the customer experience and addressing issues before they lead to churn.

How it works: AI chatbots use natural language processing (NLP) to understand and respond to customer inquiries in real time. These chatbots can handle a wide range of tasks, from answering FAQs to resolving issues related to orders or accounts. If the query is too complex for the AI, the chatbot can escalate the case to a human agent.

Benefits: By providing instant support, AI-driven customer service tools reduce wait times and enhance customer satisfaction. Customers are more likely to stay loyal to brands that offer efficient and helpful support, especially when they encounter issues.

4. Analyzing Customer Sentiment

What it is: Customer sentiment analysis uses AI to gauge how customers feel about a brand or product by analyzing feedback, reviews, and social media interactions. This helps businesses understand the emotional drivers behind customer behavior.

How it works: AI tools scan text from various sources, such as customer reviews, survey responses, and social media posts, to determine whether the sentiment is positive, negative, or neutral. These insights allow companies to track customer satisfaction and identify areas for improvement.

Benefits: Understanding customer sentiment enables businesses to address pain points and enhance the overall customer experience. If a customer expresses dissatisfaction, businesses can respond with personalized solutions, preventing churn and improving retention.

5. Offering Dynamic Incentives

What it is: Dynamic incentives involve using AI to offer personalized discounts, rewards, or promotions that align with a customer's preferences and behavior. This strategy is particularly effective for re-engaging customers who may be at risk of churning.

How it works: AI models analyze customer data to determine what type of incentive is most likely to encourage repeat purchases or continued engagement. For example, a company might offer a special discount to a customer who hasn't made a purchase in several months, or send a personalized reward to a loyal customer who frequently engages with the brand.

Benefits: By offering the right incentive at the right time, businesses can increase customer retention and encourage long-term loyalty. Dynamic incentives keep customers engaged and provide added value, which strengthens the relationship with the brand.

AI-Driven Tools for Customer Retention

There are several AI-driven tools that businesses can integrate into their customer retention efforts. These tools help companies gather valuable data, automate processes, and create more personalized experiences.

1. Customer Data Platforms (CDPs)

CDPs collect and unify customer data from various sources, such as website visits, social media interactions, and purchase history. By integrating AI into CDPs, businesses can gain deeper insights into customer behavior and preferences. This allows for more targeted retention strategies based on real-time data.

2. AI-Powered CRM Systems

Customer relationship management (CRM) systems equipped with AI can analyze customer data to predict behavior, recommend retention strategies, and automate follow-up communications. AI-driven CRM systems help businesses segment customers based on their retention risk and provide personalized recommendations for each segment.

3. Chatbots and Virtual Assistants

AI-powered chatbots and virtual assistants are essential tools for providing instant support and addressing customer needs in real time. These tools improve the overall customer experience and help retain customers by resolving issues quickly and efficiently.

4. Sentiment Analysis Tools

AI sentiment analysis tools track customer satisfaction and emotional engagement with the brand. By analyzing reviews, social media posts, and customer feedback, these tools help businesses understand how customers feel about their products or services and identify areas for improvement.

5. Recommendation Engines

Recommendation engines, powered by AI, help businesses offer personalized product or service suggestions based on customer behavior. These engines drive engagement by ensuring that customers receive relevant and timely recommendations, which encourages repeat purchases and long-term loyalty.

Measuring the Success of AI-Driven Retention Strategies

Measuring the success of AI-driven retention strategies is essential for determining their effectiveness and making data-driven improvements. Key performance indicators (KPIs) that businesses should track include:

Churn rate: The percentage of customers who stop doing business with the company over a specific period.

Customer lifetime value (CLV): The total revenue a business can expect from a customer throughout their relationship.

Repeat purchase rate: The percentage of customers who make additional purchases after their initial transaction.

Net promoter score (NPS): A measure of how likely customers are to recommend a brand to others, which indicates customer loyalty.

By tracking these metrics, businesses can assess the impact of AI on their retention efforts and continuously optimize their strategies.

The Future of AI in Customer Retention

As AI technology continues to evolve, its role in customer retention will only expand. Future AI systems will become even more accurate at predicting customer behavior, enabling businesses to intervene with personalized offers and support before customers consider leaving.

Moreover, AI's ability to analyze large datasets will improve, providing businesses with even deeper insights into customer preferences and satisfaction.

The integration of AI with advanced technologies such as machine learning, natural language processing, and predictive analytics will allow companies to develop more effective and efficient retention strategies.

The future of AI-driven customer retention is not just about keeping customers—it's about building long-term relationships that provide lasting value for both the business and the customer.

Merging AI with customer retention efforts can dramatically improve a company's ability to keep customers engaged, reduce churn, and maximize lifetime value.

AI-driven tools such as churn prediction models, personalized engagement systems, and automated customer support platforms provide businesses with the insights and automation needed to deliver exceptional customer experiences.

By proactively identifying at-risk customers, personalizing retention strategies, and continuously improving customer satisfaction, businesses can use AI to build stronger relationships and create a loyal customer base

CHAPTER 15

5 AI INNOVATIONS TRANSFORMING CUSTOMER RETENTION

Customer retention is a critical component of business success. In an age where consumers have endless choices, keeping customers loyal has become increasingly challenging.

Traditional retention strategies often rely on data analysis and customer service, but these methods are no longer enough. This is where artificial intelligence (AI) comes into play.

AI is transforming customer retention by providing businesses with powerful tools to understand customer behavior, personalize interactions, and predict future actions.

By using AI-driven insights and automation, companies can create more effective retention strategies that not only reduce churn but also increase customer loyalty and lifetime value.

In this chapter, we explore five AI innovations that are reshaping customer retention efforts, making it easier for businesses to engage their customers and build long-lasting relationships.

1. Predictive Analytics for Customer Churn

What it is: Predictive analytics uses AI to anticipate which customers are likely to stop doing business with a company. By analyzing past behavior, transaction history, and engagement patterns, AI models can identify customers at risk of churn.

How it works: AI-powered predictive models analyze customer data to detect patterns that often precede churn. For example, a drop in login frequency, a sudden decrease in spending, or less interaction with customer support might signal that a customer is losing interest in the brand.

The AI system then flags these customers, allowing businesses to take proactive steps to re-engage them.

Benefits: Predictive analytics allows businesses to act before customers churn. Instead of waiting for customers to leave, companies can offer personalized incentives, exclusive offers, or enhanced customer support to address potential concerns.

This approach helps reduce churn rates and retain high-value customers who might otherwise have been lost.

Real-World Example: Telecom companies frequently use predictive analytics to identify customers likely to switch to a competitor. By analyzing usage data, they can target these customers with special offers or loyalty programs designed to keep them engaged.

2. AI-Powered Personalization Engines

What it is: AI-powered personalization engines use customer data to tailor experiences, products, and services to individual preferences. These systems deliver personalized recommendations and content based on customer behavior, history, and preferences.

How it works: AI analyzes data from various sources, including past purchases, browsing habits, and interactions with customer service. Based on this data, the AI engine recommends products or services that match the customer's needs. It can also send personalized emails, product recommendations, and promotional offers, ensuring that each customer receives content that feels relevant and tailored to them.

Benefits: Personalization is key to customer retention because it makes customers feel valued and understood. AI-driven personalization increases engagement by showing customers the most relevant products and offers, which boosts satisfaction and loyalty. When customers consistently receive personalized experiences, they are more likely to return and make repeat purchases.

Real-World Example: Amazon's recommendation engine is a perfect example of AI-powered personalization. By analyzing user behavior, past purchases, and browsing patterns, Amazon suggests products that are highly relevant to individual customers, increasing the chances of repeat purchases and boosting customer retention.

3. AI Chatbots for Real-Time Customer Support

What it is: AI-powered chatbots provide instant, 24/7 customer support, addressing customer inquiries and resolving issues in real time. These chatbots use natural language processing (NLP) to understand and respond to customer questions.

How it works: AI chatbots can handle a wide range of tasks, from answering FAQs to assisting with complex transactions. They can instantly process customer queries, provide relevant information, and solve problems without the need for human intervention. If the issue is too complex, the chatbot can escalate the problem to a human agent.

Benefits: Real-time support is essential for keeping customers satisfied, especially in today's fast-paced digital environment. AI chatbots reduce wait times, offer consistent responses, and improve the overall customer experience. By providing immediate assistance, businesses can resolve issues before they escalate, increasing customer satisfaction and retention.

Real-World Example: Companies like Sephora and H&M use AI chatbots to assist customers with shopping questions, order tracking, and personalized recommendations. These chatbots not only provide instant support but also improve the shopping experience by offering tailored suggestions.

4. AI-Driven Sentiment Analysis

What it is: Sentiment analysis uses AI to assess customer feedback, reviews, and social media posts to gauge how customers feel about a brand or product. It helps businesses understand the emotional tone behind customer interactions and responses.

How it works: AI-powered sentiment analysis tools scan customer comments, reviews, survey responses, and social media mentions to identify whether the sentiment is positive, negative, or neutral. These tools also detect trends in customer feedback, highlighting areas where customers are consistently satisfied or dissatisfied.

Benefits: By understanding customer sentiment, businesses can address negative feedback before it leads to churn. Sentiment analysis also provides valuable insights into what customers love about a brand, allowing companies to capitalize on these strengths. Acting on customer sentiment helps businesses maintain a positive brand image and enhance customer loyalty.

Real-World Example: Sentiment analysis is widely used by brands to monitor customer feedback on platforms like Twitter and Yelp. For instance, a restaurant chain can use AI to analyze reviews and social media posts, identifying recurring issues with service or food quality. By addressing these problems promptly, the restaurant can improve customer satisfaction and reduce churn.

5. Dynamic Customer Engagement with AI

What it is: AI enables dynamic, real-time customer engagement by adapting marketing messages, offers, and interactions based on customer behavior and preferences. This innovation allows businesses to deliver personalized content across multiple channels, including email, social media, and in-app notifications.

How it works: AI systems track customer interactions in real time and adjust marketing strategies accordingly. For example, if a customer frequently browses a particular product category but hasn't made a purchase, the AI system might send a targeted discount offer or a reminder email to encourage the sale. If a customer starts to disengage, AI can trigger re-engagement efforts, such as offering a loyalty reward or a limited-time promotion.

Benefits: Dynamic customer engagement helps businesses stay connected with their customers at every stage of the customer journey. By delivering timely, relevant content, AI ensures that customers remain engaged, reducing the likelihood of churn. It also increases the chances of upselling or cross-selling products, further boosting customer retention.

Real-World Example: Streaming services like Netflix use AI to dynamically engage users by recommending shows and movies based on their viewing habits. If a user has been inactive for a while, Netflix might send a personalized email with tailored recommendations, encouraging the user to return to the platform.

The Impact of AI on Customer Retention

The five AI innovations discussed above are transforming customer retention strategies by making them more data-driven, personalized, and efficient. By using AI to predict churn, personalize interactions, provide real-time support, analyze sentiment, and dynamically engage with customers, businesses can significantly improve their retention efforts.

In the past, customer retention was reactive—businesses would wait for signs of dissatisfaction before attempting to fix the problem. Today, AI allows companies to be proactive, identifying potential issues before they arise and providing personalized solutions to keep customers satisfied.

Challenges and Considerations

While AI offers significant advantages for customer retention, businesses must also be mindful of potential challenges.

For instance, implementing AI requires access to large volumes of customer data, which raises concerns about privacy and data security. Businesses need to ensure that they are handling customer data ethically and complying with regulations like GDPR.

Additionally, AI models are only as good as the data they are trained on. If the data is biased or incomplete, AI systems might produce inaccurate predictions or recommendations. Therefore, companies need to continuously monitor and refine their AI systems to ensure they are delivering reliable results.

AI is transforming the way businesses approach customer retention by enabling more personalized, efficient, and proactive strategies.

From predictive analytics and AI-powered personalization engines to real-time chatbots and sentiment analysis, AI innovations are helping companies keep customers engaged, satisfied, and loyal.

As businesses continue to integrate AI into their retention efforts, they can build deeper connections with their customers, reduce churn, and maximize lifetime value.

In an era where customer loyalty is harder to achieve, AI offers the tools needed to create meaningful, long-lasting relationships with customers.

By embracing these AI-driven innovations, businesses can stay competitive and thrive in a customer-centric world.

CHAPTER 16

UTILIZING PUBLIC LOCATION DATA TO IMPROVE CUSTOMER INSIGHTS

In today's digital age, businesses need to leverage every possible tool to understand their customers better. One of the most valuable resources at their disposal is public location data. This data provides insights into where customers are, how they move, and what behaviors or preferences they display based on their geographic location.

By tapping into this information, companies can personalize their marketing strategies, improve customer engagement, and enhance the overall customer experience.

In this chapter, we will explore how businesses can use public location data to gain deeper customer insights, the advantages of this approach, and the ethical considerations that must be taken into account when collecting and using this information.

What Is Public Location Data?

Public location data refers to information about an individual's geographic location that can be accessed through publicly available sources. This data can come from various channels, including social media check-ins, GPS data from smartphones, location tags on photos, and information gathered by apps that require location services.

Public location data is usually anonymized to protect privacy, but it still provides valuable insights into patterns and trends. When businesses analyze this data, they can understand where their customers spend time, which places they visit, and how frequently they visit those places. This geographic context helps companies improve marketing, product offerings, and customer engagement strategies.

Why Public Location Data Is Valuable for Customer Insights

Location data provides a unique layer of understanding that can enhance traditional customer data. When combined with other information, such as demographic details and purchase history, it helps businesses build a more complete picture of their customers. Here are a few key reasons why location data is so valuable:

Understanding Customer Movement: Public location data helps businesses track how customers move throughout their day. For instance, a retail business might notice that many of its customers work in a particular area or visit a competitor's store frequently. Understanding these movement patterns enables businesses to target customers at the right time and place, increasing the chances of engagement.

Identifying Location-Based Preferences: Location data can reveal specific preferences that vary by geographic area.

For example, customers in urban areas might prefer certain products or services that differ from those in rural areas. By understanding these location-based preferences, businesses can tailor their marketing strategies and product offerings to suit the needs of each customer segment.

Improving Personalization: Personalization is a key factor in modern marketing, and location data allows businesses to take it a step further. By knowing where a customer is located, businesses can deliver more relevant and timely content, such as location-based promotions or in-store offers when a customer is nearby. This level of personalization improves the customer experience and boosts engagement.

How to Use Public Location Data to Improve Customer Insights

Here are several ways businesses can use public location data to gain insights and improve their customer strategies:

1. Segmenting Customers by Location

One of the most straightforward uses of public location data is customer segmentation. By grouping customers based on their geographic location, businesses can create targeted marketing campaigns that are more likely to resonate with specific audiences.

How it works: Location data can be used to divide customers into segments based on city, region, or even neighborhood. Businesses can then tailor their messaging, promotions, and product offerings to suit the preferences and needs of each segment.

For instance, a fashion retailer might promote winter coats to customers in colder regions while advertising summer clothing to those in warmer climates.

Benefits: Segmentation by location allows businesses to personalize their marketing efforts, making them more relevant and appealing to different customer groups. This approach leads to higher engagement rates and improved customer satisfaction.

2. Tracking Foot Traffic Patterns

Public location data can be used to track customer foot traffic patterns, helping businesses understand where their customers are spending time. This is particularly useful for brick-and-mortar stores, restaurants, and service-based businesses.

How it works: By analyzing location data from smartphones, businesses can see how often customers visit their store or a competitor's store, how long they stay, and what time of day they are most likely to visit. This information can be used to optimize store hours, plan promotions during peak times, or adjust staffing levels to better serve customers.

Benefits: Tracking foot traffic helps businesses optimize operations and marketing strategies to align with customer behavior. It also enables businesses to identify opportunities for expansion, such as opening a new location in a high-traffic area or partnering with nearby businesses for cross-promotions.

3. Enhancing Local Marketing Campaigns

Location data plays a crucial role in local marketing campaigns, enabling businesses to target customers in specific geographic areas with highly relevant messages and offers.

How it works: With geotargeting, businesses can use location data to send personalized ads, notifications, or promotions to customers based on their proximity to a store or event. For example, a restaurant could send a discount offer to customers who are within a one-mile radius during lunchtime, encouraging them to stop by.

Benefits: By using location-based marketing, businesses can drive foot traffic to their physical locations, increase brand visibility in local areas, and improve the effectiveness of their promotional campaigns.

4. Analyzing Competitive Landscape

Public location data doesn't just provide insights about your customers—it also reveals valuable information about your competitors. By analyzing location data, businesses can gain a better understanding of where competitors are located and how often customers visit them.

How it works: Businesses can track how frequently customers visit competing stores, which locations are most popular, and what factors drive foot traffic to those locations. This information can inform competitive strategies, such as opening a store in a high-traffic area where competitors are underperforming or offering promotions to attract customers away from competitors.

Benefits: Understanding the competitive landscape helps businesses make smarter decisions about location-based marketing, store placements, and promotional strategies. It also allows businesses to identify potential threats and opportunities in the market.

5. Improving Product Offerings Based on Location Data

Location data can reveal trends and preferences that vary by geographic region. Businesses can use these insights to adjust their product offerings based on what customers in different areas are most interested in.

How it works: By analyzing purchase data and location information, businesses can identify which products or services are most popular in specific areas. For example, a tech company might find that customers in urban areas are more interested in smart home devices, while rural customers prefer outdoor gadgets. This data can guide inventory decisions, product development, and localized marketing efforts.

Benefits: Tailoring product offerings to meet the preferences of customers in different regions helps businesses stay relevant and competitive. It also improves customer satisfaction by ensuring that the right products are available to the right customers.

Ethical Considerations and Data Privacy

While public location data offers significant benefits for businesses, it's important to address the ethical considerations involved in collecting and using this data. Privacy is a major concern for consumers, and businesses must ensure they handle location data responsibly.

1. Data Privacy Regulations

Businesses must comply with data privacy laws, such as the General Data Protection Regulation (GDPR) in Europe and the California Consumer Privacy Act (CCPA) in the United States. These regulations govern how companies can collect, store, and use personal data, including location data.

Best practices:

- Obtain clear consent from customers before collecting location data.

- Ensure that location data is anonymized to protect customer identities.

- Be transparent with customers about how their location data will be used and give them the option to opt out.

2. Balancing Personalization with Privacy

While customers appreciate personalized experiences, they are also concerned about how their data is used. Businesses need to strike a balance between leveraging location data for personalization and respecting customer privacy.

Best practices:

- Use location data responsibly and avoid over-targeting or invasive practices.

- Offer value in exchange for data, such as exclusive promotions or personalized recommendations, to make customers feel that sharing their location is worthwhile.

The Future of Public Location Data in Customer Insights

As technology continues to evolve, the potential for using public location data to improve customer insights will only grow. Advances in AI and machine learning will enable businesses to analyze location data more efficiently, uncovering deeper insights and creating even more personalized customer experiences.

Location-based insights will become increasingly important as businesses strive to stay competitive in a world where customers expect relevant, timely, and localized interactions. Companies that use public location data responsibly and effectively will be able to build stronger relationships with their customers, improve engagement, and drive growth.

Public location data is a powerful tool for improving customer insights. By understanding where customers are, how they move, and what preferences they have based on their location, businesses can create more targeted marketing strategies, optimize their operations, and offer personalized experiences that drive loyalty and retention.

However, businesses must also be mindful of the ethical considerations surrounding data privacy and ensure that they handle location data responsibly. As long as these principles are upheld, public location data will continue to be a valuable asset for businesses looking to deepen their understanding of their customers and gain a competitive edge in the market.

CHAPTER 17

AUTOMATING TARGETED MARKETING ACTIONS

In the fast-paced digital world, businesses must constantly adapt to meet evolving customer expectations. One of the most powerful tools that modern companies can use to stay ahead of the competition is marketing automation.

With the help of artificial intelligence (AI) and advanced analytics, businesses can now automate targeted marketing actions, ensuring that the right message reaches the right customer at the right time.

Automating targeted marketing actions not only saves time and resources but also enhances the customer experience by delivering personalized content that resonates with individual preferences. This chapter explores how marketing automation works, its benefits, and the strategies businesses can use to automate their marketing efforts effectively.

What Is Marketing Automation?

Marketing automation refers to the use of software and technology to automate repetitive marketing tasks such as email campaigns, social media posting, and customer segmentation. It allows businesses to streamline their marketing processes, personalize customer interactions, and nurture leads efficiently.

By using data-driven insights and AI, marketing automation tools can help businesses deliver targeted marketing actions that engage customers in a more meaningful and personalized way. This approach is highly effective in improving customer engagement, increasing conversion rates, and driving overall business growth.

The Role of AI in Automating Targeted Marketing

AI plays a pivotal role in automating targeted marketing actions by analyzing customer behavior, preferences, and interaction patterns. It enables marketers to segment audiences more accurately, personalize content at scale, and optimize campaigns in real-time. Here are some of the ways AI enhances automated marketing:

1. Data-Driven Segmentation

One of the most important aspects of successful marketing automation is customer segmentation. AI can analyze large volumes of customer data to identify patterns and group customers into segments based on shared characteristics, such as buying behavior, demographics, interests, or engagement levels.

How it works: AI-driven tools gather data from various sources, such as website visits, email engagement, purchase history, and social media interactions. Based on this data, AI creates customer profiles and segments that allow marketers to send highly targeted messages to each group.

Benefits: With AI-driven segmentation, businesses can deliver more relevant marketing content to specific customer segments. This increases the likelihood of engagement, as customers receive content that is tailored to their interests and needs.

2. Personalization at Scale

Consumers today expect personalized experiences from the brands they interact with. AI-powered marketing automation tools allow businesses to deliver personalized content to customers at scale, ensuring that each customer receives a message that feels tailored specifically to them.

How it works: AI analyzes customer data in real-time to create dynamic content that changes based on a customer's behavior or preferences. For example, if a customer has browsed a particular product category, AI can generate personalized product recommendations or send a follow-up email with relevant offers.

Benefits: Personalized marketing messages lead to higher engagement rates, improved customer satisfaction, and increased conversion rates. AI makes it possible to offer this level of personalization across thousands or even millions of customers, ensuring that each individual feels valued.

3. Behavioral Triggers

AI can help automate marketing actions based on customer behavior, also known as behavioral triggers. These triggers are automated responses that are initiated when a customer takes a specific action, such as abandoning a cart, browsing a certain product, or signing up for a newsletter.

How it works: When a customer interacts with a brand—whether it's visiting a website, making a purchase, or engaging with an email—AI tracks these interactions and triggers appropriate follow-up actions. For example, if a customer adds items to their cart but doesn't complete the purchase, AI can trigger an automated email reminding them of their cart, offering an incentive to complete the transaction.

Benefits: By responding to customer behavior in real-time, businesses can provide timely and relevant follow-ups, which improves the chances of converting leads into sales. Behavioral triggers also help maintain customer engagement by keeping the brand top-of-mind.

4. Optimizing Campaigns with Predictive Analytics

AI can improve the effectiveness of marketing campaigns by using predictive analytics to forecast outcomes and optimize marketing actions. Predictive analytics analyzes past data and customer behavior to predict how future campaigns will perform, allowing businesses to refine their strategies for better results.

How it works: AI tools analyze historical data from previous campaigns, including customer responses, engagement rates, and conversion outcomes. Based on this data, AI predicts which customers are most likely to engage with certain types of content or offers. It can also identify the best time to send messages or the most effective channels for engagement.

Benefits: With predictive analytics, businesses can make data-driven decisions that improve the success of their marketing campaigns. By knowing in advance which actions are likely to yield the best results, businesses can allocate resources more efficiently and focus on high-impact marketing activities.

5. AI-Driven A/B Testing

A/B testing is a method used by marketers to compare two versions of a marketing asset—such as an email, landing page, or ad—to determine which performs better. AI enhances this process by automating A/B testing and continuously optimizing marketing actions based on real-time data.

How it works: AI-powered marketing tools can automatically test multiple variations of a campaign (e.g., different headlines, images, or call-to-actions) and analyze which version performs best with specific customer segments. AI then adjusts the campaign on the fly, serving the highest-performing version to the right audience.

Benefits: Automated A/B testing powered by AI allows businesses to optimize their campaigns in real-time, ensuring that they are always delivering the most effective message to their audience. This leads to higher conversion rates and improved ROI on marketing efforts.

Benefits of Automating Targeted Marketing Actions

Marketing automation offers numerous benefits that help businesses scale their marketing efforts while delivering better results. Below are some of the key advantages of automating targeted marketing actions:

1. Increased Efficiency

Automation eliminates the need for manual tasks, such as sending emails or posting social media updates. This saves time and resources, allowing marketing teams to focus on more strategic initiatives.

With AI handling the execution of marketing actions, businesses can run campaigns more efficiently and at a larger scale.

2. Improved Customer Experience

Personalization is a key factor in enhancing the customer experience. By using AI to automate personalized marketing actions, businesses can deliver relevant content to customers at every touchpoint, improving engagement and loyalty. Customers are more likely to interact with brands that deliver content that resonates with their needs and preferences.

3. Higher Conversion Rates

Automating marketing actions based on customer behavior increases the chances of converting leads into sales. By responding to customer interactions in real-time and offering timely follow-ups, businesses can guide customers through the sales funnel more effectively, leading to higher conversion rates.

4. Data-Driven Decision Making

AI-powered marketing automation tools provide valuable insights into customer behavior, campaign performance, and overall marketing effectiveness. These insights enable businesses to make data-driven decisions that optimize their marketing strategies and improve ROI. By continuously learning from customer data, AI helps businesses refine their campaigns and deliver better results over time.

5. Scalability

As businesses grow, managing personalized marketing campaigns across a large customer base becomes increasingly difficult.

Marketing automation allows businesses to scale their efforts without compromising the quality of customer interactions. AI-driven tools can handle thousands of personalized messages simultaneously, ensuring that every customer receives a tailored experience.

Best Practices for Implementing Marketing Automation

To make the most of automated marketing actions, businesses should follow these best practices:

1. Start with Clear Objectives

Before implementing marketing automation, businesses should define clear objectives. Whether the goal is to increase conversion rates, improve customer retention, or boost engagement, having a clear focus ensures that automation efforts align with the overall marketing strategy.

2. Segment Your Audience

Effective marketing automation depends on accurate customer segmentation. Businesses should use AI-driven tools to group customers based on factors like demographics, interests, and behavior. Segmentation allows businesses to deliver more personalized and relevant content to each customer group.

3. Personalize at Every Touchpoint

Personalization is key to successful marketing automation. Businesses should ensure that every automated message, whether it's an email, social media post, or ad, is tailored to the recipient. By leveraging AI to personalize content at scale, businesses can engage customers more effectively and improve the overall customer experience.

4. Use Behavioral Triggers

Behavioral triggers are essential for automating timely marketing actions. Businesses should set up automated responses for key customer actions, such as abandoned carts, website visits, or email sign-ups. By responding to customer behavior in real-time, businesses can increase the likelihood of conversions.

5. Continuously Optimize with AI Insights

AI-driven marketing automation tools provide valuable insights into campaign performance and customer behavior. Businesses should regularly analyze these insights to optimize their strategies. Continuous optimization ensures that marketing efforts remain effective and deliver the best possible results.

Automating targeted marketing actions with AI is a powerful strategy for businesses looking to enhance their marketing efforts and improve customer engagement. By leveraging AI-driven tools, businesses can deliver personalized, relevant content to customers at the right time, increasing the chances of conversion and fostering long-term loyalty.

With benefits such as increased efficiency, improved customer experience, and higher conversion rates, marketing automation allows businesses to scale their efforts while maintaining the quality of their customer interactions. As AI technology continues to evolve, businesses that embrace automation will gain a competitive edge and drive sustainable growth in the digital age.

CHAPTER 18

THE FUTURE OF CUSTOMER ENGAGEMENT POWERED BY AI

Artificial intelligence (AI) has revolutionized the way businesses interact with their customers. From personalized marketing to predictive analytics, AI has empowered companies to engage with their audience in more meaningful and efficient ways.

As we look toward the future, AI's role in customer engagement is only expected to grow, offering new opportunities for companies to build deeper relationships with their customers and deliver even more personalized experiences.

This chapter explores the future of customer engagement powered by AI. We'll look at how AI will continue to evolve and the trends that will shape the future of customer interactions, including hyper-personalization, real-time engagement, predictive customer service, and AI-driven emotional intelligence.

The Shift Toward Hyper-Personalization

As customer expectations rise, personalization has become essential for effective engagement. In the future, AI will take personalization to the next level, moving beyond basic recommendations and tailoring every customer interaction to the individual's preferences, behaviors, and emotions.

This concept, known as **hyper-personalization**, is expected to redefine how businesses engage with their audience.

1. Real-Time Data Processing for Personalized Experiences

In the future, AI systems will be able to process customer data in real time, allowing businesses to offer personalized experiences as they happen. Imagine an online shopping experience where every product recommendation, promotion, or message is tailored to the individual in real time, based on their browsing behavior, previous purchases, and even mood.

How it works: AI will use real-time data from various sources, such as social media interactions, website visits, and app usage, to deliver personalized content at every touchpoint. For example, a customer browsing a travel website might receive personalized hotel or flight recommendations based on their search history and current location. The AI system could also adjust these recommendations dynamically as the customer interacts with the site.

Benefits: This level of hyper-personalization will create seamless, relevant, and engaging customer experiences. It will also increase customer satisfaction by delivering exactly what they need at the right time, leading to stronger customer loyalty and higher conversion rates.

2. Personalized Product and Service Development

AI will not only enhance marketing and customer interactions, but it will also influence product and service development. By analyzing customer preferences, behaviors, and feedback, AI can help companies design products and services that are personalized for specific customer segments or even individual customers.

How it works: AI will analyze large datasets from customer interactions, feedback, and social media to identify emerging trends and preferences. Businesses can use these insights to develop products that align with what their customers want. For instance, a tech company might develop personalized software features or apps based on individual user preferences and needs.

Benefits: Personalized product development ensures that companies are always aligned with customer expectations, making their offerings more appealing and relevant. This not only enhances customer satisfaction but also drives innovation in the development of new products and services.

Real-Time Customer Engagement

As AI technology advances, real-time customer engagement will become more sophisticated, enabling businesses to respond instantly to customer needs and behaviors. AI-driven tools will allow companies to engage customers in real-time across multiple channels, including websites, mobile apps, social media, and even physical stores.

1. AI-Powered Chatbots for Instant Engagement

AI-powered chatbots are already transforming customer service, but their future role in customer engagement will be even more advanced. These chatbots will become more conversational, intelligent, and emotionally aware, allowing them to engage with customers in a way that feels more human.

How it works: AI chatbots of the future will be equipped with advanced natural language processing (NLP) capabilities, enabling them to understand complex queries, detect emotional cues, and respond appropriately. For example, if a customer expresses frustration, the chatbot will recognize this emotion and adjust its tone and response to de-escalate the situation.

Benefits: AI-powered chatbots will provide instant, 24/7 support and engagement, improving the customer experience by addressing queries and resolving issues in real-time. This real-time interaction will reduce response times, increase satisfaction, and allow businesses to engage with customers at any time of the day.

2. Omnichannel Engagement

The future of customer engagement will be omnichannel, with AI allowing businesses to provide a consistent experience across multiple platforms. AI will help ensure that customer interactions remain seamless whether they happen on a website, social media platform, mobile app, or in-store.

How it works: AI will enable businesses to track customer interactions across all channels and devices. This data will allow companies to maintain a cohesive customer journey, where interactions that begin on one channel can seamlessly continue on another. For example, a customer could start a conversation with a chatbot on a company's website, then move to social media for further engagement, and later receive a personalized follow-up email based on the entire interaction.

Benefits:

Omnichannel AI engagement ensures a more connected and consistent experience, no matter where or how customers choose to engage. It also allows businesses to maintain a unified view of the customer journey, improving engagement and customer satisfaction.

Predictive Customer Service

AI will also play a major role in transforming customer service through predictive capabilities. Instead of waiting for customers to reach out with a problem, AI will allow businesses to predict potential issues before they arise and offer proactive solutions. This **predictive customer service** approach will improve customer satisfaction and retention by addressing needs before customers even realize they have them.

1. Proactive Issue Resolution

Predictive analytics will allow companies to anticipate and solve problems before they impact the customer experience. AI-driven systems will monitor customer data, usage patterns, and behaviors to detect signs of potential issues, such as a service disruption or dissatisfaction with a product.

How it works: AI tools will analyze customer interactions and product usage to predict when issues are likely to occur. For example, a telecom company might predict when a customer's internet connection is about to fail, based on usage patterns and service data. The company can then send a proactive message or schedule a service appointment before the customer experiences any disruption.

Benefits: Proactive issue resolution reduces the need for reactive customer support and ensures that problems are addressed before they escalate. This results in a smoother customer experience and strengthens the customer's trust in the brand.

2. Predictive Personalization

AI's predictive capabilities will go beyond customer service to anticipate customer needs and preferences. Predictive personalization involves using AI to forecast what a customer is likely to want next, based on their behavior and past interactions. This allows businesses to offer personalized recommendations or solutions before the customer even asks for them.

How it works: AI models will analyze customer data, such as past purchases, browsing history, and engagement patterns, to predict what customers will need in the future. For instance, an AI system might predict that a customer is likely to need a replacement product after a certain period and send a personalized offer before the product wears out.

Benefits: Predictive personalization makes customers feel understood and valued. By anticipating their needs, businesses can deliver relevant offers, products, and services, fostering long-term loyalty and engagement.

AI-Driven Emotional Intelligence

Emotional intelligence will play a crucial role in the future of customer engagement. As AI systems become more advanced, they will be able to detect and respond to human emotions with greater accuracy. This **AI-driven emotional intelligence** will allow businesses to create deeper connections with their customers by understanding and addressing their emotional states.

1. Emotion Detection and Response

AI will be capable of detecting emotions through various inputs, such as voice tone, facial expressions, and text analysis. By understanding how customers feel during interactions, AI can adjust its responses to better suit the emotional context.

How it works: AI systems will analyze speech patterns, text tone, and even visual cues from video calls to detect whether a customer is happy, frustrated, or confused. Based on this analysis, AI can adapt its tone and responses. For instance, if customer sounds upset during a call, the AI system might offer a more empathetic response or escalate the issue to a human agent for further support.

Benefits: Emotionally aware AI creates more meaningful customer interactions by addressing not only the customer's needs but also their emotions. This level of empathy improves the overall customer experience and builds stronger emotional connections between customers and brands.

2. Human-Like Conversations

In the future, AI will engage customers in conversations that feel increasingly human. These AI-powered interactions will be seamless, natural, and emotionally intelligent, allowing businesses to build rapport with their customers through conversational engagement.

How it works: AI will leverage advancements in NLP and machine learning to conduct human-like conversations with customers. These systems will understand and interpret customer queries, offer relevant solutions, and engage in back-and-forth discussions that feel organic and emotionally intelligent. Human-like AI conversations will make interactions more enjoyable for customers, fostering engagement and trust. AI's ability to engage in natural conversations will also reduce friction in customer interactions, making it easier for businesses to build long-term relationships with their audience.

The future of customer engagement powered by AI is full of exciting possibilities. From hyper-personalization and real-time engagement to predictive customer service and emotional intelligence, AI will enable businesses to connect with their customers in more meaningful and personalized ways.

CHAPTER 19

IMPROVING RETENTION THROUGH AI-ENHANCED MARKETING

One of the first and Customer retention is vital for business growth and long-term profitability. While acquiring new customers is essential, retaining existing ones often yields a higher return on investment.

Loyal customers provide consistent revenue, are more likely to recommend a brand, and cost less to maintain than acquiring new ones. However, maintaining customer loyalty in today's competitive market can be challenging. This is where artificial intelligence (AI) steps in to transform how businesses approach customer retention.

AI-enhanced marketing provides businesses with the tools to engage customers more effectively, personalize experiences, and predict churn before it happens.

By using AI, companies can craft data-driven strategies that help them not only keep their customers satisfied but also foster long-term loyalty. This chapter explores how AI can improve retention through smarter, more effective marketing efforts.

The Importance of Customer Retention

Before diving into how AI can enhance marketing for retention, it's important to understand why customer retention is critical for any business. Studies show that it can be five times more expensive to acquire a new customer than to retain an existing one. Moreover, a 5% increase in customer retention can boost profits by 25% to 95%, depending on the industry.

Loyal customers are not only valuable because of repeat purchases; they are also more likely to advocate for the brand, driving word-of-mouth referrals. Retaining customers also leads to higher customer lifetime value (CLV), which measures the total revenue a business can expect from a customer over the course of their relationship.

How AI-Enhanced Marketing Improves Retention

AI enhances customer retention strategies by providing insights that help businesses understand customer behavior, anticipate their needs, and engage them in meaningful ways. Here are several ways AI-enhanced marketing can improve retention:

1. Predictive Analytics for Retention

One of the most powerful applications of AI in marketing is predictive analytics. By analyzing historical data and current customer behavior, AI can identify patterns and predict which customers are at risk of leaving (churning).

Predictive analytics gives businesses a chance to intervene before it's too late, offering solutions that keep customers engaged.

How it works: AI models analyze customer interactions, purchase history, browsing behavior, and engagement levels to identify early signs of churn. For example, if a customer's purchasing frequency decreases or if they stop engaging with emails or social media, the AI system can flag this customer as being at risk of churning. The business can then take action by sending personalized offers, exclusive content, or targeted promotions to re-engage the customer.

Benefits: Predictive analytics allows businesses to focus their retention efforts on high-risk customers, ensuring that interventions are timely and effective. This proactive approach reduces churn rates and helps businesses retain more valuable customers, increasing overall revenue.

2. Personalization at Scale

AI allows businesses to deliver highly personalized experiences at scale, making each customer feel valued and understood. Personalization has become a key driver of customer retention, as customers are more likely to stay loyal to brands that cater to their specific needs and preferences.

How it works: AI-driven personalization involves analyzing customer data—such as purchase history, browsing patterns, and interactions across multiple channels—and using this data to deliver tailored content, product recommendations, and offers. For instance, an AI system might recommend products based on a customer's past purchases or send personalized emails with content relevant to their interests.

Benefits: Personalization increases engagement and satisfaction, as customers receive offers and recommendations that align with their preferences. This improves their experience with the brand, making them more likely to return for future purchases. AI enables businesses to scale personalization efforts, ensuring that even large customer bases receive individualized attention.

3. AI-Driven Loyalty Programs

Loyalty programs are a proven strategy for improving customer retention. AI can enhance the effectiveness of loyalty programs by analyzing customer behavior and creating personalized rewards that motivate continued engagement.

How it works: AI can analyze which rewards or incentives are most effective for different customer segments and adjust the loyalty program accordingly. For example, AI might detect that one group of customers responds best to discounts on specific products, while another group prefers access to exclusive content or services. Based on these insights, the loyalty program can be personalized to match each customer's preferences.

Benefits: AI-driven loyalty programs increase customer engagement by offering rewards that resonate with individual customers. By providing tailored incentives, businesses can keep customers engaged with the brand over the long term, encouraging repeat purchases and fostering loyalty.

4. Automating Customer Segmentation

Effective retention marketing requires targeting the right messages to the right customers. AI can automate the process of customer segmentation, allowing businesses to group customers based on shared characteristics, behaviors, and preferences.

This ensures that each segment receives relevant and timely marketing efforts.

How it works: AI-driven tools analyze customer data, such as purchase behavior, demographics, and engagement patterns, to automatically create segments based on key characteristics. These segments might include high-value customers, frequent buyers, or those at risk of churning. Once the segments are created, businesses can tailor their retention efforts to suit each group.

For example, a clothing retailer might send exclusive offers to high-value customers or provide discounts to infrequent buyers to encourage repeat purchases. AI makes it easy to target each segment with personalized campaigns that drive engagement and retention.

Benefits: Automated segmentation ensures that retention efforts are more focused and effective. Instead of sending the same message to every customer, businesses can create tailored campaigns that resonate with specific segments, increasing the likelihood of retention.

5. Optimizing Customer Engagement with AI

AI-powered tools can optimize how and when businesses engage with customers, ensuring that interactions occur at the most impactful moments. By analyzing engagement data, AI can determine the best time to send emails, launch campaigns, or offer promotions.

How it works: AI models analyze customer interactions across multiple channels, including email, social media, and website visits. Based on this data, AI systems predict when customers are most likely to engage with marketing efforts.

For example, if a customer typically opens emails in the evening, AI can schedule personalized emails to arrive at that time.

Benefits: By optimizing the timing and content of marketing interactions, AI ensures that businesses engage with customers at the right moments. This increases the effectiveness of retention efforts, improves engagement rates, and enhances the customer experience.

6. Chatbots and AI-Driven Customer Support

Customer support plays a crucial role in retention. AI-driven chatbots and virtual assistants provide instant, 24/7 customer support, ensuring that customers receive help whenever they need it. This improves the overall customer experience and reduces frustration, which can lead to churn.

How it works: AI chatbots use natural language processing (NLP) to understand and respond to customer inquiries in real time. These bots can handle a wide range of tasks, from answering common questions to resolving issues related to orders or accounts. If the issue is too complex, the chatbot can escalate the case to a human agent.

Benefits: AI-driven customer support reduces wait times and improves customer satisfaction by providing immediate assistance. By resolving issues quickly and efficiently, businesses can prevent frustration that might otherwise lead to churn.

Measuring the Success of AI-Enhanced Retention Strategies

To ensure that AI-enhanced retention strategies are effective, businesses must track key performance indicators (KPIs) that reflect customer retention and engagement. Here are a few metrics to monitor:

Churn rate: The percentage of customers who stop doing business with the company over a specific period. A lower churn rate indicates successful retention efforts.

Customer lifetime value (CLV): The total revenue a business can expect from a customer over the course of their relationship. Increasing CLV reflects strong retention and customer loyalty.

Repeat purchase rate: The percentage of customers who make additional purchases after their initial transaction. A higher repeat purchase rate signals successful engagement and retention.

Net promoter score (NPS): A measure of how likely customers are to recommend the brand to others. High NPS scores indicate strong customer satisfaction and loyalty.

By tracking these metrics, businesses can assess the impact of AI-enhanced marketing efforts on customer retention and make data-driven adjustments to improve results.

The Future of AI in Customer Retention

As AI continues to evolve, its role in customer retention will only grow. Future AI systems will become even more adept at predicting customer behavior, personalizing experiences, and optimizing engagement.

Additionally, advances in machine learning and natural language processing will enable businesses to deliver even more sophisticated and personalized marketing efforts.

AI will also continue to integrate with other emerging technologies, such as augmented reality (AR) and the Internet of Things (IoT), allowing businesses to engage with customers in new and innovative ways. For example, AI-powered AR apps might offer personalized product recommendations based on a customer's surroundings or preferences.

The future of AI-enhanced marketing promises to make customer retention strategies smarter, more effective, and more engaging, helping businesses build long-lasting relationships with their customers.

AI-enhanced marketing is transforming how businesses approach customer retention. By leveraging predictive analytics, personalized experiences, AI-driven loyalty programs, and automated segmentation, companies can improve customer retention rates and build stronger, more loyal customer relationships.

CHAPTER 20

THE BROADER IMPACT OF AI ON CUSTOMER RETENTION

Artificial intelligence (AI) is rapidly reshaping the way businesses interact with their customers. While AI is often associated with automation and efficiency, its most transformative power lies in enhancing customer retention.

The ability to keep customers engaged and loyal over the long term is crucial for business success. Through AI, companies can better understand customer behavior, personalize interactions, predict churn, and make real-time decisions that directly impact retention.

The broader impact of AI on customer retention goes beyond simply keeping customers engaged—it influences marketing, customer service, and even product development.

In this chapter, we'll explore how AI is driving change in customer retention and examine the key areas where AI is making the most significant impact.

Why Customer Retention Matters in the AI Era

Customer retention has always been a critical factor for business success, but its importance has intensified in today's competitive market. Retaining customers is far more cost-effective than acquiring new ones, and loyal customers often provide more long-term value. AI enhances retention strategies by providing data-driven insights that help businesses anticipate customer needs and address them proactively.

Companies using AI for customer retention can better understand their customers, personalize interactions at scale, and automate engagement. The result is a more responsive and customer-centric approach to business, which leads to higher satisfaction, loyalty, and revenue growth.

1. Predictive AI and Proactive Customer Retention

One of the most impactful applications of AI in customer retention is predictive analytics. Predictive AI allows businesses to forecast future customer behavior, such as the likelihood of churn, based on historical data and real-time insights. By predicting when a customer is likely to leave, businesses can intervene proactively, offering personalized incentives or solutions to keep them engaged.

How Predictive AI Works

AI analyzes large volumes of customer data, including past interactions, purchase patterns, engagement levels, and even social media activity. By identifying trends and patterns in this data, AI models can predict future behavior. For example, a customer who has reduced their engagement with the brand or hasn't made a purchase in several months might be flagged as at risk of churn. The business can then take preemptive action, such as offering a discount or personalized service.

Benefits of Predictive AI

Proactive engagement: Predictive AI allows businesses to engage with at-risk customers before they leave, reducing churn and increasing customer retention.

Targeted interventions: Instead of using a blanket approach to retention, AI enables companies to target specific customers with tailored offers, improving the effectiveness of retention efforts.

Improved customer experience: By addressing issues or offering incentives before a customer becomes dissatisfied, companies can create a more positive experience, strengthening loyalty.

2. Hyper-Personalization at Scale

AI enables hyper-personalization, a more advanced form of personalized marketing that tailors every interaction to an individual's preferences, behaviors, and needs. In the context of customer retention, hyper-personalization means delivering content, offers, and messages that resonate with customers on a deeper level, keeping them engaged with the brand.

How AI Drives Hyper-Personalization

AI analyzes real-time customer data from various sources, such as browsing behavior, purchase history, location data, and even social media activity.

It then uses this information to create personalized recommendations, product suggestions, or targeted messages. For example, an AI-driven system might send a special offer for a product a customer has been browsing but has not yet purchased, or recommend related products based on their buying habits.

Benefits of Hyper-Personalization

Increased engagement: Customers are more likely to engage with personalized content that speaks directly to their interests and needs.

Stronger loyalty: When customers feel understood and valued, they are more likely to remain loyal to the brand over time.

Enhanced customer satisfaction: Hyper-personalization helps businesses deliver a more relevant and enjoyable experience, which improves overall customer satisfaction and retention.

3. AI-Powered Loyalty Programs

AI is revolutionizing loyalty programs by making them smarter and more dynamic. Traditional loyalty programs reward customers based on transactions, but AI can take this a step further by analyzing customer behavior to personalize rewards and offer incentives that match their preferences.

How AI Enhances Loyalty Programs

AI-powered loyalty programs analyze customer data to understand what motivates individual customers to stay engaged. Based on this data, AI can offer personalized rewards, such as discounts on frequently purchased items, early access to new products, or special promotions on a customer's birthday.

AI can also optimize loyalty programs by identifying which rewards are most effective for different customer segments. For example, frequent shoppers might prefer discounts, while infrequent buyers might respond better to exclusive content or limited-time offers. AI makes it easy to tailor rewards and incentives to different customer groups, driving higher engagement and retention.

Benefits of AI-Driven Loyalty Programs

Tailored rewards: Personalized loyalty programs encourage repeat business by offering rewards that resonate with each customer's preferences.

Increased engagement: AI-powered programs keep customers engaged by offering timely and relevant incentives, making them more likely to return.

Data-driven optimization: AI can continually refine loyalty programs based on customer behavior, ensuring that rewards are both appealing and effective.

4. Real-Time Customer Support with AI

AI-driven chatbots and virtual assistants are transforming customer support by providing real-time assistance to customers, addressing issues as they arise, and improving overall satisfaction. For retention, responsive customer support is critical, as unresolved issues often lead to frustration and churn.

How AI Improves Customer Support

AI-powered chatbots use natural language processing (NLP) to understand and respond to customer queries in real-time. These chatbots can handle a variety of tasks, from answering simple questions to resolving more complex issues related to orders or services. For example, a chatbot might assist a customer in tracking their order, processing a return, or offering product recommendations based on their browsing history.

If the issue is too complex for the AI to handle, the chatbot can escalate the problem to a human agent, ensuring that the customer gets the help they need as quickly as possible.

Benefits of AI-Driven Customer Support

24/7 availability: AI-powered support ensures that customers can get help at any time, improving satisfaction and reducing frustration.

Instant responses: Quick issue resolution leads to happier customers and reduces the likelihood of churn.

Cost efficiency: AI-driven support reduces the need for human agents, lowering operational costs while maintaining high service levels.

5. AI-Driven Customer Sentiment Analysis

Understanding customer sentiment is crucial for improving retention. AI-driven sentiment analysis tools can help businesses gauge how customers feel about their brand by analyzing data from customer reviews, social media posts, and survey responses. This allows companies to identify dissatisfied customers early and take corrective action before they churn.

How Sentiment Analysis Works

AI systems scan customer-generated content, such as reviews, social media posts, and feedback surveys, to identify positive, negative, or neutral sentiments.

By analyzing the tone and context of the content, AI can determine how customers feel about specific products, services, or interactions with the brand.

For example, if a customer leaves a negative review about a product, the AI system can flag it for further investigation, allowing the company to reach out and resolve the issue.

Benefits of AI-Driven Sentiment Analysis

Proactive engagement: Identifying negative sentiment early enables businesses to take corrective action before customers decide to leave.

Improved customer experience: By addressing pain points and resolving issues, businesses can improve customer satisfaction and retention.

Real-time feedback: Sentiment analysis provides real-time insights into how customers feel, allowing companies to adapt their strategies quickly.

6. AI and the Customer Journey

AI has the potential to optimize the entire customer journey, from the moment a customer first interacts with a brand to their ongoing engagement. By analyzing customer behavior at each stage of the journey, AI can help businesses identify areas for improvement, streamline processes, and ensure a seamless experience.

How AI Enhances the Customer Journey

AI analyzes data from every touchpoint—website visits, email openings, social media interactions, and purchases—to gain a holistic view of the customer journey. It then uses this data to personalize interactions, optimize marketing efforts, and automate follow-ups. For instance, if a customer abandons their cart, AI can trigger an automated email reminder with a personalized offer to encourage them to complete the purchase.

AI can also identify points of friction in the customer journey, such as slow response times or complicated checkout processes, and suggest improvements to enhance the overall experience.

Benefits of AI-Optimized Customer Journeys

Seamless interactions: AI ensures that customers have a consistent and personalized experience across all touchpoints.

Reduced friction: By identifying and addressing pain points, AI improves the customer experience, leading to higher retention.

Continuous improvement: AI-driven insights help businesses refine their strategies and optimize the customer journey over time.

The broader impact of AI on customer retention is profound, touching every aspect of how businesses engage with and retain their customers. From predictive analytics and hyper-personalization to AI-powered loyalty programs and real-time customer support, AI is transforming how companies build lasting relationships with their customers.

As AI technology continues to advance, businesses that embrace these tools will be able to create more personalized, proactive, and responsive retention strategies. The result is not only reduced churn but also stronger customer loyalty, higher satisfaction, and long-term business success. AI is not just the future of customer retention—it is the present, and companies that leverage its power will thrive in an increasingly competitive market.

CHAPTER 21

STRENGTHENING YOUR BUSINESS WITH AI-LED EXPERIMENTS

In today's fast-paced and data-driven market, businesses must constantly evolve to remain competitive. One of the most effective ways to drive innovation and growth is through experimentation.

However, traditional experimentation methods can be time-consuming and resource intensive. Artificial intelligence (AI) is transforming how businesses conduct experiments by enabling faster, more accurate, and scalable testing. AI-led experiments allow companies to make data-driven decisions, optimize their strategies, and strengthen their overall performance.

This chapter will explore how AI-led experiments can strengthen your business by improving decision-making, reducing risk, and accelerating innovation.

We'll also discuss key areas where AI-driven experimentation can be applied, and how businesses can implement AI experimentation to enhance growth.

What Are AI-Led Experiments?

AI-led experiments involve using artificial intelligence to run tests, analyze data, and provide insights that drive strategic decisions. These experiments typically involve testing multiple variables (such as product features, marketing messages, pricing strategies, and customer segments) to determine which combinations produce the best results.

Unlike traditional experiments, which can take weeks or months to conduct, AI can run thousands of tests simultaneously and analyze results in real-time.

By leveraging AI, businesses can optimize their strategies faster and with greater accuracy, allowing them to experiment with various approaches before committing significant resources. AI-led experiments are not limited to marketing or product development—they can be applied to all areas of a business, including operations, customer service, and supply chain management.

Why AI-Led Experiments Are Crucial for Business Growth

AI-led experiments provide businesses with a competitive edge by enabling rapid testing and optimization. Here's why AI-driven experimentation is essential for strengthening your business:

1. Data-Driven Decision Making

In the past, many business decisions were based on intuition or incomplete data. AI-led experiments remove guesswork by providing data-driven insights that allow businesses to make more informed decisions. AI analyzes vast amounts of data quickly, identifying trends, patterns, and correlations that might be missed by human analysts.

How it works: AI models can simulate different scenarios, test multiple hypotheses, and predict outcomes based on historical data. For example, a retailer might use AI to experiment with various pricing strategies, testing different price points and discount levels to see how they impact sales volume and profitability.

Benefits: Data-driven decision-making leads to better outcomes, reducing the risk of costly mistakes. By relying on objective data rather than gut instincts, businesses can be more confident in their decisions and adapt their strategies based on real-world results.

2. Increased Speed and Efficiency

Traditional experiments can take weeks or months to complete, but AI can accelerate the process by running tests in parallel and processing results in real-time. This speed allows businesses to iterate quickly, refining their strategies based on immediate feedback.

How it works: AI-driven experimentation platforms can run multiple tests simultaneously, analyzing different variables (such as customer segments, marketing channels, and product features) at the same time. For example, an e-commerce business might use AI to test various homepage designs, product recommendations, and checkout processes all at once.

Benefits: By speeding up experimentation, AI enables businesses to optimize their strategies faster and capitalize on new opportunities before competitors. This ability is particularly important in industries where consumer preferences and market conditions change rapidly.

3. Reduced Risk

Experimentation often involves risk, especially when testing new ideas, products, or strategies. AI reduces this risk by allowing businesses to test multiple hypotheses in a controlled environment before scaling them up.

How it works: AI can simulate different scenarios, providing businesses with insights into potential risks and rewards. For example, a company considering a major product launch might use AI to run simulations of market reactions, pricing strategies, and customer feedback, reducing the risk of failure by identifying the most promising approach.

Benefits: By minimizing the risk associated with experimentation, AI allows businesses to innovate with greater confidence. Companies can test bold ideas without the fear of negative consequences, leading to more innovative and effective strategies.

4. Personalization and Customer Insights

AI-led experiments allow businesses to test different approaches to personalization and customer engagement, optimizing strategies to meet individual customer needs and preferences.

How it works: AI can run personalized experiments by analyzing customer data and testing various personalization techniques. For example, an AI system might test different email subject lines, product recommendations, or marketing messages to determine which approach resonates best with different customer segments.

Benefits: Personalized experiences drive customer loyalty and engagement. AI-led experiments enable businesses to continuously refine their personalization strategies, ensuring that they are always delivering the most relevant and impactful experiences to their customers.

Key Areas Where AI-Led Experiments Strengthen Businesses

AI-led experiments can be applied across various business functions, from marketing and product development to customer service and operations. Here are some key areas where AI experimentation can deliver significant benefits:

1. Marketing Optimization

AI-led experiments can dramatically improve the effectiveness of marketing campaigns by testing different messages, channels, and target audiences. With AI, marketers can experiment with different ad formats, content types, and promotional strategies to find the best combination that drives engagement and conversions.

Example: An online retailer might use AI to test various email marketing campaigns, experimenting with different subject lines, send times, and personalization techniques. The AI system can analyze the results of each experiment in real-time and automatically adjust the campaign based on which version performs best.

Benefits: AI-driven marketing experiments increase the efficiency of campaigns, reduce wasted ad spend, and improve conversion rates. Businesses can reach the right customers with the right message at the right time, maximizing the impact of their marketing efforts.

2. Product Development and Innovation

AI-led experiments can accelerate product development by testing different product features, designs, and pricing strategies. Companies can use AI to experiment with various versions of a product before launching it to the market, ensuring that they are offering the most appealing and competitive product possible.

Example: A software company might use AI to test different user interfaces (UI) for its application, analyzing which design leads to higher user satisfaction and engagement. The AI system can collect data from user interactions and adjust the UI based on feedback, optimizing the product before it is fully released.

Benefits: AI-driven product experimentation leads to better products that are more aligned with customer needs. By testing features and designs before launch, businesses can reduce the risk of product failure and increase the likelihood of market success.

3. Customer Experience Enhancement

Customer experience is a key driver of retention and loyalty. AI-led experiments can be used to improve the customer experience by testing different service models, communication strategies, and engagement techniques.

Example: A telecom company might use AI to experiment with different customer support models, testing chatbots, live agents, and hybrid approaches to see which provides the best customer experience. AI can analyze customer feedback, service times, and resolution rates to determine which approach is most effective.

Benefits: AI-driven experimentation allows businesses to continuously refine the customer experience, ensuring that they are meeting customer expectations and delivering superior service.

4. Supply Chain and Operations Optimization

AI-led experiments can also be applied to operational processes, helping businesses optimize their supply chain, logistics, and inventory management. By testing different operational strategies, companies can improve efficiency, reduce costs, and minimize delays.

Example: A manufacturing company might use AI to experiment with different supply chain models, testing various sourcing strategies, inventory levels, and shipping methods to determine the most cost-effective and efficient approach. AI can analyze the results of each experiment and provide recommendations for optimizing operations.

Benefits: AI-driven experimentation in operations leads to improved efficiency, reduced costs, and more reliable supply chain management. Businesses can respond more quickly to market changes and ensure that their operations are running smoothly.

Best Practices for Implementing AI-Led Experiments

To make the most of AI-led experiments, businesses should follow these best practices:

1. Define Clear Objectives

Before conducting AI-led experiments, businesses should have clear objectives. Whether the goal is to improve customer engagement, optimize a product feature, or reduce operational costs, having a well-defined goal ensures that the experiments are aligned with the company's overall strategy.

2. Start Small and Scale

Businesses should start with small-scale experiments before scaling them up. By testing different approaches on a smaller scale, companies can gather insights and refine their strategies before rolling them out to a larger audience.

3. Leverage Real-Time Data

AI-led experiments rely on real-time data to provide accurate and actionable insights. Businesses should ensure that their data collection processes are robust and that they are gathering relevant data from customer interactions, transactions, and other key touchpoints.

4. Continuously Iterate and Improve

AI-led experiments are most effective when they are part of an ongoing process. Businesses should continuously iterate on their experiments, using AI insights to refine their strategies and improve over time. By regularly testing new ideas and approaches, companies can stay ahead of the competition and adapt to changing market conditions.

AI-led experiments offer businesses an unprecedented opportunity to strengthen their strategies, optimize operations, and drive growth. By enabling rapid testing, data-driven decision-making, and personalized customer experiences, AI allows businesses to experiment with confidence and innovate faster than ever before.

Whether applied to marketing, product development, customer service, or operations, AI-driven experimentation empowers businesses to test new ideas, reduce risk, and continuously improve